Sadlier

CHRIST IN US ™

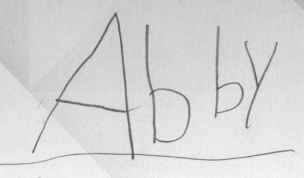

Parish Edition 3

Abby

"*Christ In Us* Grade 3 cover artwork speaks to the children's discovery of their interactions with friends and schoolmates."

Reverend Donald Senior, C.P., S.T.D.

Sadlier Religion

This advanced publication copy has been printed prior to final publication and pending ecclesiastical approval.

Acknowledgments

This publication was printed with permission pending from the following copyright holders.

Excerpts from the *Catechism of the Catholic Church, second edition,* © 2000, Libreria Editrice Vaticana—United States Conference of Catholic Bishops, Washington, D.C. All rights reserved.

Scripture texts in this work are taken from the *New American Bible, revised edition* © 2010, 1991, 1986, 1970 Confraternity of Christian Doctrine, Washington, D.C. All Rights Reserved. No part of the New American Bible may be reproduced in any form without permission in writing from the copyright owner.

Excerpts from the English translation of *The Roman Missal* © 2010 International Commission on English in the Liturgy, Inc. (ICEL). All rights reserved.

Excerpts from the English translation of *Rite of Penance* © 1974, ICEL. All rights reserved.

Excerpts from *The Order of Confirmation.* Copyright © 2016 ICEL. All rights reserved.

Excerpts from *Rite of Baptism for Children.* Copyright © 1969 ICEL. All rights reserved.

Quotations from papal addresses, audiences, homilies, speeches, messages, meditations, encyclicals, and other Vatican documents are from www.vatican.va and copyright © by Libreria Editrice Vaticana or Secretaria pro Communicatione.

Copyright © 2020 by William H. Sadlier, Inc. All rights reserved. This book, or any part thereof, may not be reproduced in any form, or by any means, including electronic, photographic, or mechanical, or by any sound recording system, or by any device for storage and retrieval of information, without the written permission of the publisher.

Printed in the United States of America.

S® and Sadlier Religion® are registered trademarks of William H. Sadlier, Inc. All rights reserved.

CHRIST ᴵᴺ US™ is a trademark of William H. Sadlier, Inc.

William H. Sadlier, Inc.
9 Pine Street
New York, NY 10005-4700

ISBN: 978-0-8215-3693-3

1 2 3 4 5 6 7 8 9 WEBC 23 22 21 20 19

Cover Series Design: Silver Linings Studios; **Cover Series Illustrator:** Jui Ishida.

Photo Credits

age fotostock/Caia Image/Robert Daly: 14; DreamPictures/VStock: 21 *top*; Juice Images: 19; KidStock: 32, 254. Alamy Stock Photo Agency/Design Pics Inc: 148; Godong: 82; RosaIreneBetancourt 7: 51; Torontonian: 72; Giuseppe Ciccia: 24, 256; Florian Kopp: 73 *bottom*, 250; Steve Skjold: 189; Marmaduke St. John: 150, 213, 215; Marmaduke St. John: 158; Hero Images Inc.: 119; Lexington Herald-Leader/ZUMAPRESS.com: 179; Tetra Images: 161; Visions of America, LLC: 97; ZUMA Press Inc: 95; Zuma Press, Inc.: 230. Bridgeman Images/Brooklyn Museum of Art: 31; Nativity, 1917 (fresco), Montenard, Frederic (1849-1926)/Église Saint François de Sales, Paris, France: 46; Pentecost, 1732 (oil on canvas), Restout, Jean II (1692-1768)/Louvre, Paris, France: 23; The Amazing Love of Jesus, Uptton, Clive (1911-2006)/Private Collection/© Look and Learn: 64. Brooklyn Museum/Purchased by public subscription/James Tissot: 86. Karen Callaway: 21 *bottom*, 53, 54, 80, 89, 96, 121 *top*, 165, 172, 180. The Crosiers/Gene Plaisted, OSC: 44, 45, 48, 88, 247 *bottom*; 253. Diocese of Tyler Office of Communications: 78. Getty Images/Des: 149; JoSon: 181, 7; terrababy: 203 *bottom*; Westend61: 195; Ty Allison: 137; Ariel Skelley: 6, 98; Donat Sorokin: 73 *top*; Caiaimage/Paul Bradbury: 35; eDEA/A. DAGLI ORTI : 22. GoodSalt/Lars Justinen: 163; Lifeway Collection: 55, 105, 120, 173, 197 *bottom*, 227 *bottom*, 233 *top*; Pacific Press: 178; Providence Collection: 219; The Classic Bible Art Collection: 221. Greg Lord: 85. iStockphoto.com: 231; alacatr: 190 *bottom*; Alex: 107, 212; alexhstock: 201; asiseeit: 217; bedo: 200; cstar55: 193; den-belitsky: 208–209 *bottom*; eyetoeyePIX: 169; FatCamera: 155; ffennema: 138; fstop123: 116; gradyreese: 182; Highwaystarz-Photography: 187; Imagesbybarbara: 113; JBryson: 229; karenpritchett: 115; kevron2001: 214–215 *bottom*; koleskikovserg: 218; konradlew: 211; kumeda: 191 *top*; LuminaStock: 104;

Milan_Jovic: 27; nicolesy: 145; NikonShutterman: 153; princessdlaf: 130, 209 *top*; RapidEye: 224; RomoloTavani: 194; samxmeg: 188; sedmak: 136; sharply_done: 127; skiserge1: 147; skynesher: 94, 225; sprokop: 232–233 *bottom*; Tempura: 29; valentinrussanov: 103; vdesign77: 43; VikahSuh: 251 *background*; Westhoff: 157; XiXinXing: 123; Chris Hepburn: 206; Africa Studio: 166; monkeybusinessimages: 140, 223; Morsa Images: 174. Newscom/GODONG/picture-alliance/Julian Kumar: 90. Laura Reischour: 79. Shutterstock.com/alefbet: 112; buchan: 237, 238, 239 *bottom*, 247 *top*, 249; bymuratdeniz: 135; jorisvo: 128; karelnoppe: 111; Lopolo: 28; Macrovector: 196–197 *top*, 202–203 *top*, 220–221 *top*, 226–227 *top*; mattjeacock: 170; Millionstock: 52; Redcollegiya: 190–191 *bottom*, 208–209 *background*, 214–215 *background*, 232–233 *background*, 235 *background*; Slanapotam: 18, 60, 102, 144, 186; unguryanu: 132; Wassenbergh: 131; Zvonimir Atletic: 207; Diego Cervo: 162; Dan Costa: 154; Mikael Damkier: 114; Nataliya Dolotko: 235 *background*; Phillip B. Espinasse: 38; Iakov Filimonov: 129; Mike Mareen: 20; Audrius Merfeldas: 239 *top*; ANURAK PONGPATIMET: 36; Rick Schroeppel: 177; Steve Snowden: 66; Romolo Tavani: 39, 252; Green Flame: 236; JHDT Productions: 205; Real CG Animation Studio: 199; Syda Productions: 12; wavebreakmedia: 11. Spirit Juice Studios: 37, 40, 56, 70, 77, 87, 108, 248, 255. SuperStock/age fotostock/Spencer Grant: 65; age fotostock/Chico Sanchez: 74; age fotostock/Jim West: 61; Caia Images: 93; Cultura Limited: 69; F1 ONLINE/Jürgen Ritterbach: 62. W.P. Wittman Limited: 30, 63, 71, 106, 121 *bottom*, 139, 146, 156, 164, 171.

Illustrator Credits

Steve James: 17, 59, 101, 143. Robert Kayganich: 240–241. Jim Madsen: 10, 13, 25, 33, 41, 47, 49, 57, 67, 75, 83, 91, 99, 109, 117, 125, 133, 141, 159, 167, 175, 183, 237, 243, 244, 244, 245, 246. Jim Madsen: 10, 13, 25, 33, 41, 47, 49, 57, 67, 75, 83, 91, 99, 109, 125, 141, 159, 167, 175, 183, 237 *top*, 243, 244, 244, 245, 246.

Christ In Us was developed in collaboration with the wisdom of the community. The team included respected catechetical, liturgical, pastoral, and theological experts who shared their insights and inspired its development.

With grateful acknowledgment of
William Sadlier Dinger and Frank Sadlier Dinger
for their leadership, vision, and commitment to excellence in the development
of Sadlier's catechetical programs and resources since 1963

Theological and Liturgical Consultants

Most Reverend Christopher James Coyne
Bishop of Burlington, VT

Donna Eschenauer, Ph.D.
Associate Dean, Associate Professor of
    Pastoral Theology
St. Joseph's Seminary and College

Rita Ferrone, M.Div.

Thomas Kendzia
Sadlier National Consultant for
    Liturgy and Music

Reverend Monsignor John Pollard, M.Ed., S.T.L.

Alissa Thorell, M.T.S

John B. Angotti, M.A.P.S.

Barbara Sutton, D.Min.

Kathleen Dorsey Bellow, D.Min.

Scripture Consultant

Reverend Donald Senior, C.P., S.T.D.
Chancellor and President Emeritus
    Catholic Theological Union

Catechetical Consultants

Amy Welborn, M.A.

Susan Stark

Sr. Theresa Engel, O.S.F.
Member of the School Sisters of St. Francis

Maureen A. Kelly, M.A.

Karla Manternach, M.A.

Woodeene Koenig-Bricker, M.A.

Connie Clark

Shannon Chisholm, Ph.D.

Susan M. Sink

Maureen Shaughnessy, S.C.

Lori Dahlhoff, Ed.D.

Andrea D. Chavez-Kopp, M.Ed.

Educational Consultants

Richard Culatta

Heidi Hayes Jacobs, Ed.D.

Jay McTighe

Allie Johnston

Learning Style Inclusion Consultants

Charleen Katra, M.A.

Jennifer Ochoa, M.Ed., LDT/C

Inculturation Consultants

Luis J. Medina
Director, Bilingual Catechesis

Charlene Howard, M.A.

Michael P. Howard, M.A.
Eat the Scroll Ministry

Catholic Social Teaching

Kristin Witte, D.Min.

Genevieve Jordan Laskey, M.A.

Michael Jordan Laskey, M.A.

Media and Technology Consultants

Spirit Juice Studios

Top Floor Productions

Sr. Caroline Cerveny, S.S.J.-T.O.S.F., D.Min.

Reviewers and Contributors

Jennifer Hayhurst

Concetta M. Duval, Ed.D.

Trenton W. Mattingly, M.A.

Debi Mahr, M.A.

Mary Homola, M.A.

Linda Mele Dougherty, M.A.

Mary Jane Krebbs, Ph.D.

Darcy Osby, M.Div.

Hugh M. Keenan

Sadlier Consultant Team

Steven Botsford
Senior Director of Digital Catechesis

Suzan Larroquette, M.T.S.
Senior Director of Catechetical Consultant Services

Kathleen Hendricks, M.A.
National Catechetical Consultant Contributing Writer

John Collins, M.Ed.
National Religion Consultant

Writing/Development Team

Diane Lampitt, M.Ed.
Vice President, Product Manager, Religion

Blake Bergen
Vice President, Religion Editorial

Deacon Matthew Halbach, Ph.D.
Senior Catechetical Director

Regina Kelly, M.A.
Editorial Director, Religion

Gloria Shahin, M.A.
Senior Editorial Director, Religion

Mary Carol Kendzia, M.S.
Research and Development Director, Religion

Robert Vigneri, M.S.
Executive Editor, Religion

Editorial Staff

Tina Dennelly, Linda Nicholson, Roger Ochoa,
Amanda Pisciotta

Publishing Operations Team

Patricia Coryell
Senior Vice President & Publisher

Kevin Feyen
Vice President, Shared Services

Carole Uettwiller
Vice President, Supply Chain

Vince Gallo
Senior Creative Director

Francesca O'Malley
Art/Design Director

Cesar Llacuna
Senior Image Manager

Roderick Gammon
Senior Director, Digital Strategy

Toby Carson
Digital Design Director

Cheryl Golding
Senior Production Director

Laura Reischour
Project Manager

Evie Alvarez
Program Manager

Jovito Pagkalinawan
Electronic Prepress Director

Yolanda Miley
Image Rights & Permissions Director

Lucy Rotondi
Business Manager

Design/Image Staff

Kevin Butler, Nancy Figueiredo, Stephen Flanagan,
Debrah Kaiser, Gabriel Ricci, Bob Schatz,
Daniel Sherman

Production Staff

Robin D'Amato, Carol Lin, Vincent McDonough,
Allison Pagkalinawan, Brad Tucker

Contents

Catholic Spirituality 10

Welcome 11

Unit 1: What Do We Believe?
The Faith Professed
Unit Opener 17

Lesson 1: How do we know God? 19

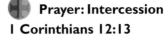 **Prayer: Traditional**

Genesis 1:31

• All of creation shows us God's goodness. • The Bible is God's Word. • Jesus shows us the way to God the Father. • The Holy Spirit guides the Church.

Lesson Test: Show What You Know

Partners in Faith: Venerable Pierre Toussaint

Mini-Task: How do I tell others about God?

At Home: Pray a family Bible verse.

Lesson 2: Who is God? 27

Prayer: *Lectio* and *Visio Divina*

Matthew 3:16–17

• We can know God through creation. • God revealed himself as One God in Three Divine Persons. • Jesus is the Son of God and God himself. • Jesus and the Holy Spirit strengthen and guide the Church.

Lesson Test: Show What You Know

Partners in Faith: Saint John the Baptist

Mini-Task: How does the Blessed Trinity guide me?

At Home: Show others who you are.

Lesson 3: Why did God make us? 35

Prayer: Praise

John 15:15

• Creation shows the glory of God. • Faith is a gift from God. • We sin when we choose to disobey God. • The Church helps us live in God's friendship forever.

Apostles' Creed

Lesson Test: Show What You Know

Partners in Faith: Saint Augustine

Mini-Task: How can I live in God's friendship?

At Home: Mass prepares us to live in peace.

Lesson 4: Who is Jesus Christ? 43

Prayer: Litany

The Mystery of Faith, *Roman Missal*

• The Holy Spirit prepared Mary to be the Mother of Jesus. • In the Incarnation, the Son of God became man. • Jesus died on the Cross to save us from sin. • Jesus Christ ascended to heaven and will come again at the end of time.

Lesson Test: Show What You Know

Partners in Faith: Saint Joseph

Mini-Task: How is Jesus Christ with me today?

At Home: Notice the details in a crucifix.

Lesson 5: What is the Church? 51

Prayer: Intercession

1 Corinthians 12:13

• Christ is the Head of his Body, the Church. • Jesus is with us in the Church. • The Church is one, holy, catholic, and apostolic. • The pope and bishops are the successors of the Apostles.

Lesson Test: Show What You Know

Partners in Faith: Saint Nicholas

Mini-Task: How can I spread the Good News about the Church?

At Home: Discuss other Catholic churches you have visited.

Unit 2: How Do We Celebrate What We Believe?
The Faith Celebrated

Unit Opener **59**

Lesson 6: How does God share his life with us? **61**

 Prayer: Meditation

Matthew 18:20

• In the liturgy, the Church participates in Jesus' saving work. • Jesus and the Holy Spirit prepare us to receive grace. • Jesus gave the Church the sacraments. • Sacramentals prepare us to receive God's grace.

Lesson Test: Show What You Know

Partners in Faith: Saint Dominic Savio

Mini-Task: How can I share God's love and joy with others?

At Home: Jesus heals, forgives, and nourishes us.

Lesson 7: How do we praise and thank God? **69**

Prayer: Thanksgiving

Genesis 2:3

• The Mass is the most important way we celebrate the Lord's Day. • The Church celebrates Jesus' life and saving work all year long. • All around the world, Catholics use their local customs to praise and worship God. • Devotions draw us closer to God.

Lesson Test: Show What You Know

Partners in Faith: Saint Gregory the Great

Mini-Task: How do I respond to God's Word?

At Home: Attend Mass as a family.

Lesson 8: How do we become members of the Church? **77**

Prayer: Thanksgiving

Homily of Pope Francis

• The Sacraments of Initiation welcome us into the Church. • In Baptism we are born to new life in Christ. • Confirmation completes our Baptism • The Eucharist is the heart of the Church's life.

Lesson Test: Show What You Know

Partners in Faith: Saint Katharine Drexel

Mini-Task: What does it mean to me that I am a member of the Church?

At Home: We are close to Jesus at Mass.

Lesson 9: How do we celebrate God's forgiveness and healing? **85**

Prayer: *Lectio* and *Visio Divina*

Luke 15:6

• We celebrate Jesus' forgiveness and healing in the Church today. • We ask forgiveness in Jesus' name. • In the Sacrament of Penance, the Church forgives us in Jesus' name. • In the Sacrament of Anointing of the Sick, the Church prays for the healing of those who are suffering.

Lesson Test: Show What You Know

Partners in Faith: Saint Padre Pio

Mini-Task: How do I celebrate God's forgiveness?

At Home: Read the Parable of the Prodigal Son.

Lesson 10: How are we strengthened for service to God and others? **93**

Prayer: Intercession

Luke 4:18

• All members of the Church share in Christ's mission. • Bishops, priests, and deacons teach and guide the Church. • Matrimony is a Sacrament at the Service of Communion. • We call our family a "church of the home."

Lesson Test: Show What You Know

Partners in Faith: Blessed Stanley Rother

Mini-Task: What does God's strength help me to do?

At Home: Thank those in your family who have helped you.

Unit 3: How Do We Live What We Believe?
The Faith Lived
Unit Opener 101

Lesson 11: How do we know God loves us? 103

✚ **Prayer: Thanksgiving**

James 1:17

• God wants us to share in his life and love. • We are called to care for one another. • God gives us freedom to choose what is good and holy. • The natural law is written in our hearts.

Lesson Test: Show What You Know

Partners in Faith: Blessed Anne-Marie Javouhey

Mini-Task: How can I share in God's work?

At Home: God gives us many gifts to share with the world.

Lesson 12: How do we respond to
God's love? 111

✚ **Prayer: Blessing**

John 15:9

• Good moral choices help us to live in God's Kingdom. • A well-formed conscience helps us choose what is morally good. • Virtues are good spiritual habits. • The Church works for justice and peace.

🔊 **Beatitudes**

Lesson Test: Show What You Know

Partners in Faith: Blessed Pier Giorgio Frassati

Mini-Task: How do the Beatitudes help me respond to God's love?

At Home: Live the Beatitudes in your daily life.

Lesson 13: How does God teach us
to love? 119

✚ **Prayer: Meditation**

Romans 7:12

• God's laws are divinely revealed. • The commandments call us to love God above all else. • The commandments call us to love and respect ourselves and others. • The Church teaches and guides us.

🔊 **Ten Commandments**

Lesson Test: Show What You Know

Partners in Faith: Saint Alphonsus Liguori

Mini-Task: How do the commandments help me share God's love?

At Home: Family rules help us support each other.

Lesson 14: What turns us away from
God's love? 127

✚ **Prayer: Petition**

Penitential Act, Roman Missal

• Original Sin affects all people. • Sin harms our relationship with God and one another. • Some sins break our friendship with God. • Making the wrong moral choices can lead to serious sins.

Lesson Test: Show What You Know

Partners in Faith: Blessed Anne Mary Taigi

Mini-Task: How can I make good choices?

At Home: Small, wrong choices can lead to serious sin.

Lesson 15: What turns us toward
God's love? 135

✚ **Prayer: Lectio and Visio Divina**

Acts of the Apostles 15:11

• We are called to be Jesus' disciples. • Grace is a gift God gives to us out of love. • God's grace helps us choose what is morally good. • Sanctifying grace makes us holy.

Lesson Test: Show What You Know

Partners in Faith: Saint Benedict

Mini-Task: What turns me toward God's love?

At Home: We are strengthened by God's grace.

Unit 4: How Do We Become What We Believe?
The Faith Prayed
Unit Opener 143

Lesson 16: What is prayer? 145

✚ **Prayer: Praise**

Psalm 145:18

• We join with the Church in prayer. • We can pray with the Psalms. • Prayer brings us closer to God. • The Church prays to God the Father.

🔊 **Psalm 23**

Lesson Test: Show What You Know

Partners in Faith: Saint Gertrude the Great

Mini-Task: How does prayer help me be closer to God?

At Home: Pray from the Book of Psalms.

Lesson 17: Why do we pray? 153

✚ **Prayer: Petition**

James 5:16

• The Holy Spirit helps us to pray. • Prayer teaches us to trust God. • Prayer helps us to be Jesus' disciples. • The Church is called to pray always.

Lesson Test: Show What You Know
Partners in Faith: Saint Edith Stein
Mini-Task: What do I ask God for in prayer?
At Home: Pray a prayer of petition for help.

Lesson 18: How do we pray?................161
⊕ **Prayer: Intercession**
Philippians 4:6–7
• The Church helps us bless, praise, and trust in God.
• The Church is always at prayer. • We pray together in the Liturgy of the Hours. • We can pray aloud and in the silence of our hearts.
Lesson Test: Show What You Know
Partners in Faith: Saint Alberto Hurtado
Mini-Task: How can I pray every day?
At Home: Pray for those who are in need.

Lesson 19: What helps us to pray?............169
⊕ **Prayer:** *Lectio* and *Visio Divina*
Eucharistic Prayer 2, *Roman Missal*
• The Communion of Saints is united in prayer. • We pray with the Word of God and the liturgy. • We learn to pray in our families. • Prayer helps our faith grow.

Lesson Test: Show What You Know
Partners in Faith: Julian of Norwich
Mini-Task: How do the saints help me pray?
At Home: Thank God by praying "hosanna."

Lesson 20: Why is the Lord's Prayer called the perfect prayer?..........................177
⊕ **Prayer: Traditional**
Pope Benedict XVI
• The Lord's Prayer is the perfect prayer. • Jesus taught us to call God our Father. • In the Lord's Prayer we praise and honor God. • We trust God to care for us, body and soul.
🔊 **The Lord's Prayer**
Lesson Test: Show What You Know
Partners in Faith: Saint John Bosco
Mini-Task: How does praying the Lord's Prayer help me follow Jesus?
At Home: Think of your favorite words or phrases from the Our Father.

Unit 5: Why and How Do We Celebrate the Church Year?
Unit Opener............................185

Lesson 21: The Church Year
How do we celebrate Jesus Christ?.............187
Prayer Ritual

Lesson 22: Advent
Why does Jesus come to save us?..............193
Readers Theater

Lesson 23: Christmas
How did the Son of God enter human history?...........................199
Readers Theater

Lesson 24: Lent
How are we called to repentance today?.......205
Prayer Ritual

Lesson 25: Triduum
Why did Jesus die on the Cross and rise again?............................211
Prayer Ritual

Lesson 26: Easter
How is the Risen Jesus present in his Church?..........................217
Readers Theater

Lesson 27: Pentecost
Who is the Holy Spirit?.....................223
Readers Theater

Lesson 28: Ordinary Time
How do we grow as Jesus' followers?.............................229
Prayer Ritual

Christ In Us Sourcebook.....................235

Family Companion.......................251

Glossary...............................257

Q&A..................................260

Index.................................266

Your Spiritual Journey

Christ In Us offers a saint or holy person for every grade. The Holy Person for Grade 3 is Venerable Pierre Toussaint. As you journey through each unit, remember to pray to Venerable Pierre. Ask him to guide you to be closer to Jesus Christ.

Pierre Toussaint was born in 1766 in a French colony now known as Haiti. Pierre worked as a house slave on a plantation. He was raised Catholic and was educated as a child. In 1787, he moved to New York City with the family that owned him.

In 1807, Pierre was granted his freedom. Pierre began to work as a hairdresser and soon became famous for his skills. Pierre eventually became a rich man. But he knew that true happiness can only be found in following Jesus and his teachings. Together with his wife, Pierre founded an orphanage to care for homeless children. He also helped raise money to build a new Catholic church in New York City, now known as Old St. Patrick's Cathedral.

Pierre showed his devotion to God by the way he lived. He gave money and time to many organizations serving the poor.

Pierre died in 1853 at age 87. He was buried in the cemetery at the church he had helped to build. In 1991, his body was moved to Saint Patrick's Cathedral on Fifth Avenue in New York.

In 1996 Pierre was declared Venerable, the first step to sainthood. Pierre's life serves as a model of holiness to us all.

Welcome to **Christ In Us**, an exciting way to grow in your Catholic faith!

Each one of us is on a journey to love and know Jesus Christ. Imagine if every person who met you knew you were a friend of Christ!

Together in this program:

we will **ENCOUNTER** Jesus Christ

we will **ACCOMPANY** him in our lives

we will **WITNESS** to our faith.

You will use this book as well as your online digital portal as you discover and grow closer to Jesus Christ.

As you journey in your faith, you can think about these questions:

It is Christ in you; the hope for glory.

Colossians 1:27

Why is it important to have Christ live in you?

What would happen if you did not have Jesus in your life?

How do your faith, the Church, and your family help bring you closer to God?

Every lesson has four Spiraling Main Ideas.
Here is an example.

Each lesson has one or more **Faith Words** to help you understand the language of our Catholic faith.

Be sure to look at all the wonderful photos and beautiful art found in the pages of your book.

As you explore this question, you might be asked to stop and think more about it, and then do a short **Activity** to answer it better.

You will be asked to **Show What You Know** by writing the answers to some short questions pertaining to the lesson.

All of creation shows us God's goodness.

God created the whole universe out of nothing. Everything God has created, from waterfalls to tiny grains of sand on the beach, from plants to people, tells us about him and his goodness.

Often, God finds ways to speak to us through creation. We read in the Bible about Noah and the ark. After the great flood, when Noah, his family, and all of the animals left the ark and found dry land, God made a special promise, called a **covenant**, with Noah. He promised to love and care for everything he had made, including all of us, forever. God used his own creation—a rainbow—as a sign of his promise.

Faith Word

covenant an agreement between God and his people

How do I show God's goodness to the world?

Did You Know?

 The Bible was first printed in 1455.

Activity

Use the following words to write or use a storyboard to tell the story of Noah and the ark. Read or tell your story to a friend.

God   Noah   ark   rain   covenant   flood   animals   rainbow

You will not be alone as you journey through **Christ In Us**. You will have lots of **Partners in Faith**—saints and other holy people who lived amazing lives—walking with you.

Along with Venerable Pierre Toussaint, here are some other Partners in Faith whom you will meet throughout the book!

Saint Joseph

Saint Gertrude the Great

Saint John the Baptist

Saint Edith Stein

Saint Nicholas

Saint Katharine Drexel

Blessed Pier Giorgio Frassati

Blessed Anne Mary Taigi

Next, you will be asked to go to your **Portfolio** to creatively share how you can bring Christ to the world.

Each lesson ends with a **Mini-Task** that invites you to show ways you can live out your faith as a missionary disciple of Christ.

Finally, you will be given ways to think and talk with your family **At Home**.

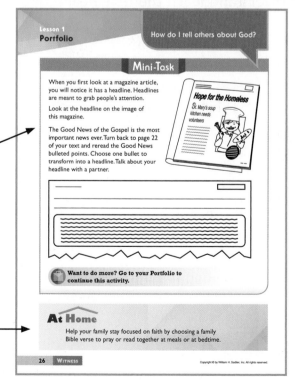

Christ In Us features an online portal filled with exciting media and activities to go with the lessons in your book. If you see one of these icons below in your book, you know it's time to visit the student portal for more. (Note: Not every icon will appear in your book.)

 Participate in lesson prayers, whose words are online and downloadable

Learn more about the lesson's **Did You Know?** topic by watching an interesting video and doing an activity

 Learn more about the lesson's **Partner in Faith** by watching an online video and completing the activity that follows

Listen to Scripture verses and Catholic prayers and learn them by heart

Find fun activities to share and recall what you have learned

Show What You Know by completing online assessments

Read and remember the **Faith Words** definitions

Complete projects and tasks in the online **Portfolio** or *Portfolio Workbook*

Listen to the songs for your grade level and sing along!

Your Songs for Grade 3	
Unit Songs	**Liturgical Catechesis Seasonal Songs**
Unit 1: "We Have Been Told," David Haas	**Church Year:** "Forever Will I Sing," Ed Bolduc
Unit 2: "Light of Christ," Tom Kendzia	**Lent:** "Lead Us to the Water: Gathering," Tom Kendzia
Unit 3: "I Send You Out," John Angotti	**Triduum:** "I Have Loved You," Michael Joncas
Unit 4: "Here I Am, Lord," Dan Schutte	**Ordinary Time:** "Prayer of St. Francis," Sebastian Temple
Unit 5: "We Are Called," David Haas	

Your journey continues with your login to *Christ In Us* Digital!

Here you can explore all the exciting resources that blend together with your textbook.

Take a look at your personalized online dashboard. Everything you need is at your fingertips!

- Think of your portfolio as your digital backpack! Here you can get your assignments, see reminders, send emails, and even talk to your catechist.

- Interactive Mini-Tasks enable you to share exciting activities with others. You will be able to get hands on and creative by making videos or interactive posters.

- Listen with your heart and pray the prayers of *Lectio* and *Visio Divina*, praise, petition, intercession, adoration, and blessing from your lesson.

- Track your progress with digital quizzes and tests.

Have a wonderful year!

Unit 1
The Faith Professed

Jesus Is Baptized

Unit Prayer

Leader: Venerable Pierre Toussaint exemplifies what it means to live a life of faith rather than just use words that are good and holy. In doing so, he modeled how we should "be the Church" instead of just going to church, to live as the light of Christ.

Let us listen to how it is possible to live "as the Church." Listen to the stories of missionary disciples today.

Leader: Let us pray:
Jesus, we know that you want us to be your eyes and hands in the world by the way we treat each other. For help in living in your light, we pray:

Reader: Help us to lift up the poor and lonely.

All: We will bring your light and peace.

Reader: Help us to care for those who hunger and thirst.

All: We will bring your light and peace.

Reader: Help us to lead those in darkness into your light.

All: We will bring your light and peace.

Reader: Guide our feet on your path of love for all.

All: We will bring your light and peace.

Leader: Following the example of Venerable Pierre Toussaint, we say:
Make us models of your love.

All: Make us models of your love.

End the Unit Prayer by singing the unit song.

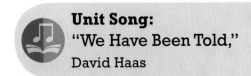

Unit Song:
"We Have Been Told,"
David Haas

Missionary Discipleship

Can you remember a time when someone helped you when you were lonely or when you felt afraid? What happened? How did you feel when you were helped? How have you helped others when they needed you?

How do we know God?

God is the Creator of everything. God made everything we can see and everything we cannot see. He existed before anything else existed. We can know God and live as his children. God gives us so many ways to know him. We can know God by seeing his wonderful creation. We get to know him from what he tells us in the Bible. We can know him through the Church. We can especially know God as the Blessed Trinity through Jesus.

Go to the digital portal for a traditional prayer.

"God looked at everything he had made, and found it very good." Genesis 1:31

All of creation shows us God's goodness.

God created the whole universe out of nothing. Everything God has created, from waterfalls to tiny grains of sand on the beach, from plants to people, tells us about him and his goodness.

Faith Word

covenant an agreement between God and his people

Often, God finds ways to speak to us through creation. We read in the Bible about Noah and the ark. After the great flood, when Noah, his family, and all of the animals left the ark and found dry land, God made a special promise, called a **covenant**, with Noah. He promised to love and care for everything he had made, including all of us, forever. God used his own creation—a rainbow—as a sign of his promise.

How do I show God's goodness to the world?

Did You Know?

 The Bible was first printed in 1455.

Activity

Use the following words to write or use a storyboard to tell the story of Noah and the ark. Read or tell your story to a friend.

God   Noah   ark   rain   covenant   flood   animals   rainbow

The Bible is God's Word.

Creation alone does not tell us everything about God. God loves us so much that he wants to speak to us. God speaks to us through the Bible. The Bible is also called Sacred Scripture. The Bible is God's own Word.

God chose people to write the Bible. God the Holy Spirit inspired and guided the people who wrote the Bible. He gave them freedom to write in their own way. We read about events, signs, stories, lessons, and prayers in the Bible. The Bible is a collection of books about God's love for us. The Bible tells us about our call to live as God's people.

God the Holy Spirit guides our minds and hearts to believe all that God is telling us. The Holy Spirit guides the Church to teach us truthfully about what God wants us to know.

Jesus shows us the way to God the Father.

God tells us about himself in the Bible. Jesus, God the Son, fully shows us who God is. Everything Jesus said and did shows us his love for his Father and the Father's love for us.

In the New Testament, the **Gospels** tell us about Jesus and his words and deeds. The word *gospel* means "good news." Here is what the Good News means for us:

- Jesus is the Son of God. He came into the world to become one of us and to save us. He came to show us God's love for us.

- Everything Jesus did—his teachings, his miracles, his love for everyone, his prayers, and especially his Death and Resurrection—shows us the way to God the Father.

- Jesus is the Savior of the whole world. All of us have been saved by the **Paschal Mystery**: Jesus' Passion, or suffering, Death, Resurrection, and Ascension.

- Jesus is our Risen Lord. He is lives at the right hand of the Father in heaven. He is always with us by the power of the Holy Spirit!

The Gospels were written after Jesus' Resurrection and Ascension, when he returned to his Father in heaven. The four Gospel writers are called the four Evangelists.

Faith Words

Gospel the Good News that we are saved by Jesus Christ, the Son of God

Paschal Mystery the Passion, Death, Resurrection, and Ascension of Jesus Christ

Their four names are the names of the Gospels: Matthew, Mark, Luke, and John.

The four Gospels are at the beginning of the New Testament. The Gospels are so important because they tell us about Jesus, who fully reveals God to us.

Activity

Write one way you can share the Good News.

_____

_____

_____

The Holy Spirit guides the Church.

"When the time for Pentecost was fulfilled, they were all in one place together. And suddenly there came from the sky a noise like a strong driving wind, and it filled the entire house in which they were. Then there appeared to them tongues as of fire, which parted and came to rest on each one of them. And they were all filled with the holy Spirit and began to speak in different tongues, as the Spirit enabled them to proclaim" (Acts of the Apostles 2:1–4).

Faith Word

Sacred Tradition
the ways the Church continues to pass on everything that God revealed to us in Jesus Christ

The Holy Spirit came to the Apostles, Mary, and the other disciples on Pentecost. The Holy Spirit guided the Apostles to begin the work Jesus gave them. They shared the Good News of Jesus with all people. God worked through the Apostles and their followers. Since the time of the Apostles, the Church has continued to share the preaching and teachings of Jesus Christ.

The Church teaching of all that God has revealed in Jesus Christ is called **Sacred Tradition**.

God reveals himself to us in both Sacred Scripture and Sacred Tradition. Through Sacred Tradition the Holy Spirit guides the Church to pass on what God has revealed in the Bible and the teachings of the Apostles. Tradition includes creeds, or statements about what we believe. These statements tell about how we worship God and follow Jesus' teachings.

Scripture and Tradition present God's revelation to us. Together, they show us that the Holy Spirit is alive in the Church through all time, until Jesus comes again in glory.

Sacred Tradition refers to Jesus' teachings, ministry, and authority as they were passed down to his Apostles and their successors, the bishops.

The Holy Spirit lives in the Church, which is the Body of Christ on earth. You are part of the Church. You can live out Jesus' words and teachings every day. As Catholics, we all work together as one Church, one Body in Christ, to help spread the Good News about Jesus.

Faith Words

covenant   Gospel   Sacred Tradition
Paschal Mystery

 Show What You Know

Match the term to the correct definition.

1. Sacred Tradition
2. gospel
3. Paschal Mystery
4. covenant
5. Sacred Scripture

Jesus' Passion, Death, Resurrection, and Ascension

a special promise made by God

God's own Word in the Bible

a word that means "good news"

the ways the Church passes on everything that God revealed in Jesus Christ

Partners in Faith

Venerable Pierre Toussaint

Venerable Pierre Toussaint was a slave. He learned to be a hairdresser. He was such a good hairdresser that he earned enough money to buy his freedom. He gave to the poor and helped raise money to build a church in New York City.

 Learn more about the life of Venerable Pierre Toussaint.

Copyright © by William H. Sadlier, Inc. All rights reserved.

Mini-Task

When you first look at a magazine article, you will notice it has a headline. Headlines are meant to grab people's attention.

Look at the headline on the image of this magazine.

The Good News of the Gospel is the most important news ever. Turn back to page 22 of your text and reread the Good News bulleted points. Choose one bullet to transform into a headline. Talk about your headline with a partner.

Hope for the Homeless

St. Mary's soup kitchen needs volunteers

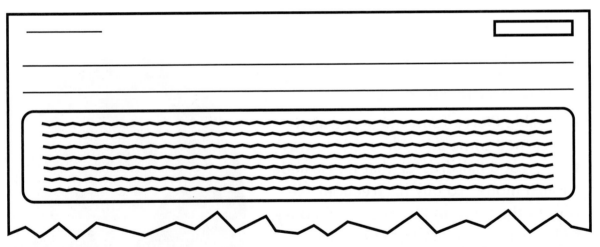

 Want to do more? Go to your Portfolio to continue this activity.

At Home

Help your family stay focused on faith by choosing a family Bible verse to pray or read together at meals or at bedtime.

Copyright © by William H. Sadlier, Inc. All rights reserved.

Who is God?

All four Gospels tell us that the people who saw Jesus' baptism heard a voice from heaven. The Holy Spirit came down like a dove. This was one way God revealed who he is: the Father, the Son, and the Holy Spirit.

We may not be able to see and hear God in the same way the people at Jesus' baptism did. We can read, hear, and understand God's own Word in the Bible and in the teachings of the Church. These are ways God tells us who he is.

Go to the digital portal for a *Lectio* and *Visio Divina* prayer.

"He saw the Spirit of God descending like a dove [and] coming upon him. And a voice came from the heavens, saying, 'This is my beloved Son.'" Matthew 3:16–17

We can know God through creation.

When people know you, they might know your name or what grade you are in. Someone who knows you a little better might know your birthday and what you like to do. Someone who knows you really well might know what makes you happy, sad, or afraid. Knowing *about* you and really *knowing* you are different things.

The same is true for God. We can know about him, but knowing God deep in our hearts is different. God is a mystery. That means we need some help to truly get to know and love him.

Who is someone who knows me well?

Did You Know?

The Sign of the Cross is used in many ways.

Little by little, God revealed his good and loving plan for us to get to know him. God loves us so much that he comes first to us. He loves us so much that he has a plan to help us know him. His plan began with creating the world out of nothing.

Over time, God fully revealed his love by sending us his Son, Jesus, who gives us our best understanding of God. And through the Holy Spirit, Jesus gave us the Church, so that all people in all times can know and love God.

Activity

Write one thing you know about God right now.

Tell a friend how you know this.

Write one thing about God that you'd like to know more about.

What I Know	How I Know This	What I Want to Know

Faith Word

Blessed Trinity God the Father, God the Son, and God the Holy Spirit are One God in Three Persons

God revealed himself as One God in Three Divine Persons.

God showed us that he is One God in Three Persons: God the Father, God the Son, and God the Holy Spirit. This is something we cannot understand on our own. We know it and believe it because God revealed it. God tells us this in the Bible and in the Church, and God does not lie.

The Church calls this mystery of One God in Three Persons the **Blessed Trinity**. The Gospels and the Church teach us that the Blessed Trinity is three equal and divine Persons. The Persons of the Blessed Trinity have always existed and always will.

The Blessed Trinity is a mystery that is at the heart of our faith! We may not be able to see the Trinity the same way we can see the people around us. Yet we can see the Trinity at work in our lives. We see God's love in the world in many ways, including in the beauty of creation, in children helping their families, and in people taking care of the sick.

Each Divine Person of the Trinity has a special role. God the Father, God the Son, and God the Holy Spirit show us how much God loves and cares for us.

Jesus is the Son of God, and God himself.

The Gospels tell us that one day Jesus came to a river called the Jordan. John the Baptist saw Jesus coming toward him and said:

"Behold, the Lamb of God, who takes away the sin of the world. He is the one of whom I said, 'A man is coming after me who ranks ahead of me because he existed before me.' . . . Now I have seen and testified that he is the Son of God" (John 1:29–34).

John the Baptist knew Jesus was the Savior whom God promised to send. John also knew that the Savior whom God sent was both human and divine. He said that Jesus "is the Son of God."

Jesus is the Son of God and the son of Mary. He is both God and man. He is our Savior who lived, died, and rose again to save us from our sins. Jesus is the Second Person of the Blessed Trinity. He was born and lived among us as one of us. Jesus felt joy, sadness, and pain the same way that we do. Jesus was like us in every way except sin.

Jesus and the Holy Spirit strengthen and guide the Church and her members.

Jesus sent his disciples out to heal the sick and preach about God. He told them the Blessed Trinity would be with them. He said, "For it will not be you who speak but the Spirit of your Father speaking through you" (Matthew 10:20).

Jesus speaks of the Holy Spirit, the Third Person of the Blessed Trinity. We sometimes call the Holy Spirit our Advocate. An advocate is someone who works on someone else's behalf. Through the Holy Spirit, Jesus gives us the Church, so that all people in all times can know and love God. The Holy Spirit unites and guides the whole Church and helps her members grow in holiness.

The Holy Spirit also works within each of us by helping us live in God's love. The Holy Spirit helps us to grow in holiness. When we are **holy**, we love God. When we are living in God's love, we are holy. We are following Jesus' example of loving God and others. The Holy Spirit helps us respond to God's great love for us and to love God and others perfectly.

Faith Word

holy growing in God's love and sharing it

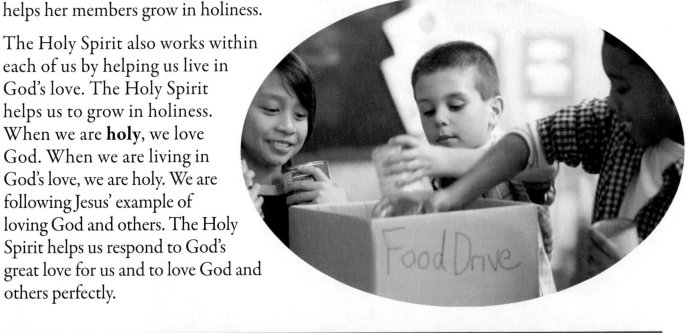

Activity

The Holy Spirit helps you love God and others. Write a short prayer to the Holy Spirit on the banner. Have a friend say the prayer with you.

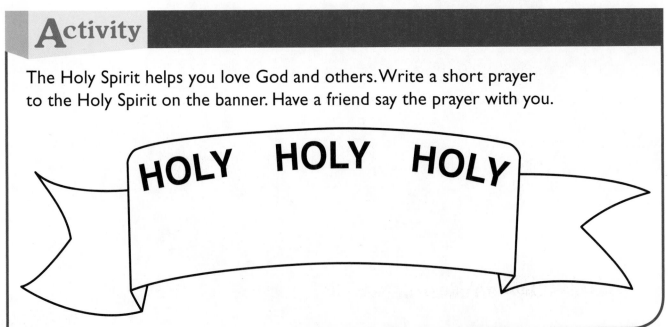

HOLY HOLY HOLY

Faith Words

Blessed Trinity   **holy**

 ## Show What You Know

Put an X next to the correct answers.

1. The _____ is One God in Three Persons.

☐ Blessed Trinity | ☐ Body of Christ

2. Jesus is the _____ Person of the Blessed Trinity.

☐ Second | ☐ Third

3. When we are _____, we grow in God's love and share it with others.

☐ heavenly | ☐ holy

4. The Blessed Trinity is a _____ of our faith.

☐ mystery | ☐ message

5. Jesus and the _____ strengthen and guide the Church and her members.

☐ People of God | ☐ Holy Spirit

Partners in Faith

Saint John the Baptist

Saint John the Baptist helped people prepare for Jesus. He baptized people and told them to be sorry for their sins. He told them to do good deeds. John recognized Jesus as the Son of God.

 Learn more about the life of Saint John the Baptist.

Copyright © by William H. Sadlier, Inc. All rights reserved.

Mini-Task

Each Divine Person of the Blessed Trinity has a special role. God the Father, God the Son, and God the Holy Spirit reveal the love of the Blessed Trinity for all people.

God the Father sent the Holy Spirit to help us live like his Son, Jesus. The Holy Spirit never leaves us and always helps us live as Jesus' followers.

Use the story map to tell when the Holy Spirit showed you how to love God and others.

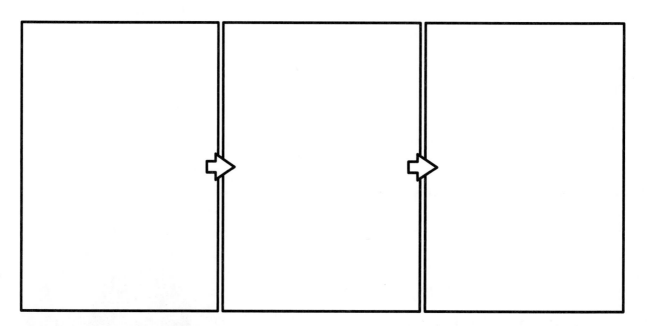

 Want to do more? Go to your Portfolio to continue this activity.

We all want to be known for who we are. Talk as a family about some ways you can show others who you are.

Copyright © by William H. Sadlier, Inc. All rights reserved.

Why did God make us?

Jesus told us why God made us. God wants us to live in friendship with him always. When we live in God's friendship, we find happiness deep in our hearts. We will live forever with God in perfect joy and peace. God gives us the gift of faith to know him. Faith helps us trust God and believe in every truth he has revealed.

 Go to the digital portal for a prayer of praise.

"I have called you friends, because I have told you everything I have heard from my Father."

John 15:15

Creation shows the glory of God.

Everything God has created is good. The stars, mountains, oceans, trees, puppies, and even the tiniest ants are all good. And God has created people—like you! You are part of God's creation, made in God's own image. That makes *you* good.

Faith Word

glory greatness or honor

There is no end to God's goodness. God's unending goodness is his **glory**. All of creation shares in God's glory. God wants us to share in this glory and live in his friendship. Friendship with God is what makes us happy, deep in our hearts.

What are some things that make me happy?

Did You Know?

All living creatures show God's goodness.

Activity

Psalms are prayer-songs. Write a psalm thanking God for having created you in his image. Include the words *faith*, *glory*, and *friend*. Recite your psalm to your family.

_____

_____

_____

Faith is a gift from God.

Most of us enjoy giving gifts to our friends as much as we enjoy receiving them. So imagine how much God enjoys giving us gifts. God has given us the gift of faith to help us know him better and grow in our friendship with him. Faith is what helps us believe and trust in God. Faith is powerful because it is from our all-powerful God. It allows us to believe what we cannot see or touch. We are free to accept God's gift of faith and choose how we will act on it.

We express our faith in God whenever we gather at Mass. We stand and profess one of the creeds of our Church. Creeds are statements of all that we believe. In the Creed, we affirm our belief in the Trinity and in the Church. When we profess the Creed, we are reminded that we are Jesus' followers.

We believe all that Jesus teaches. We are his Church. We do not just say these words. We go out and live them! Before leaving Mass, we hear these words: "Go in peace, glorifying the Lord by your life" (*Roman Missal*).

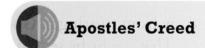 **Apostles' Creed**

Every day we can choose to follow Jesus. We do this by following Jesus' example of loving God and others. But we do not do it alone. Jesus has promised that God is always with us. God the Father sent his Son, who gave us the Church. The Church can also help us at every step of our lives. Because the Church is the Body of Christ, Jesus is always with us, guiding us. We also call the Church the temple of the Holy Spirit. The Holy Spirit is always with the Church. The Holy Spirit unites the Church and gives the Church life.

We gather at Mass to pray as a Church, to listen to God's Word, and to receive Jesus himself in the Sacrament of the Eucharist. We find ways to love God and others as Jesus taught us. God is with us in the Sacrament of Penance and Reconciliation. We confess our sins. We ask for and receive God's forgiveness. In these and many other ways, we can live forever where we are meant to be: in God's friendship.

Activity

We do many things as the Body of Christ that help us know and love God. Check the things you do as a member of the Church that help you know and love God.

Circle one thing you want to do this year that you are not doing right now.

Action	Yes! I do this.
Go to Mass	
Pray	
Give to a food bank	
Go to Confession	
Receive Holy Communion	
Help a neighbor	

Faith Words

glory   **Original Sin**

 Show What You Know

Fill in the blanks with the words in the Word Bank.

disobey   faith   Original Sin   friendship   glory

1. All of creation takes part in God's _____ .

2. God wants us to live in his _____ .

3. _____ is the first sin, committed by Adam and Eve.

4. _____ is what helps us believe in and trust God.

5. Sin is a choice to _____ God.

Partners in Faith

Saint Augustine

Saint Augustine was not very interested in religion as a young man. His mother, Saint Monica, prayed and prayed that he would change. He began to read the Bible and listen to teachers of the faith. He was sorry for his sins. He changed his life and became a priest. He told everyone that God will always forgive us if we are sorry.

 Learn more about the life of Saint Augustine.

Copyright © by William H. Sadlier, Inc. All rights reserved.

Mini-Task

God made us to love him and others. But sometimes we do things that hurt our relationship with God and others.

Disciples need to be able to know the difference between actions that help or hurt our friendship with God.

Work with a partner.

Design a scenario in which two characters do something that hurts their friendship with God and others.

Then change that scenario to make it one that helps their friendship with God and others.

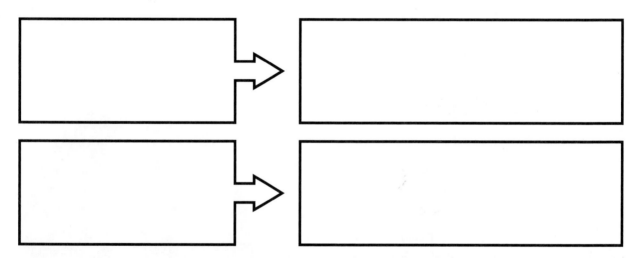

 Want to do more? Go to your Portfolio to continue this activity.

 At Home

Talk with your family about how Sunday Mass prepares us to "go in peace," glorifying God. What is one way you can do this as a family?

Copyright © by William H. Sadlier, Inc. All rights reserved.

Who is Jesus Christ?

Jesus is the Savior of the world. He died on the Cross for our sins. He rose from the dead to bring us eternal life with God the Blessed Trinity in heaven. Jesus is both God and man. We can get to know Jesus by learning about his life and his teachings. We can also get to know Jesus by learning about his mother, Mary.

Go to the digital portal for a litany prayer.

"Save us, Savior of the World, for by your Cross and Resurrection you have set us free."
The Mystery of Faith, Roman Missal

The Holy Spirit prepared Mary to be the Mother of Jesus.

God the Father chose Mary to be the mother of his only Son. The Holy Spirit filled Mary with the graces to help her for this wonderful—and at times, very difficult—job. Mary's faith in God was strong and pure. She always did what she knew God wanted her to do. She accepted everything that came from God, even if she didn't fully understand.

When the angel visited Mary and asked if she would be the Mother of God, Mary was confused. How could she be the Mother of God?

"And the angel said to her in reply, 'The holy Spirit will come upon you, and the power of the Most High will overshadow you. Therefore the child to be born will be called holy, the Son of God . . . for nothing will be impossible for God.' Mary said, 'Behold, I am the handmaid of the Lord. May it be done to me according to your word'" (Luke 1:35–38).

Mary's words "I am the handmaid of the Lord" show her complete faith and trust in God. We give Mary many titles to honor her and to teach about her Son, Jesus. One of her titles is the Blessed Virgin. This title means that God alone is the Father of Jesus. It also teaches us that Mary did not have any more children.

Mary carried Jesus in her womb, just as any mother carries her baby. Mary and Joseph raised Jesus in their home in Nazareth. Everything Mary did followed God's plan for his Son, Jesus. Jesus, Mary, and Joseph are called the Holy Family.

What do I think God has planned for me?

Did You Know?

Mary is the first disciple.

Activity

We use many different names to honor Mary. Here are some titles we give her. Write a short prayer using your favorite name. Draw a picture to go along with the prayer.

Mother of God

Queen of Heaven

Mother of Sorrows

Help of the Sick

Star of the Sea

Untier of Knots

Mother of Mercy

In the mystery of the Incarnation, the Son of God became man.

Saint Luke's Gospel tells us about Jesus' birth in the city of Bethlehem.

"While they were there, the time came for her to have her child, and she gave birth to her firstborn son. She wrapped him in swaddling clothes and laid him in a manger, because there was no room for them in the inn" (Luke 2:6–7).

A manger is a trough, or box, that holds food for animals in a stable. The manger where Mary laid the baby Jesus was probably in a type of shelter, or cave. People kept animals they tended, such as sheep, goats, or oxen, in stables. The Bible tells us there was no room anywhere else for them. Why would God choose such a place for his own Son's birth? Wouldn't a palace be better for the Son of God?

Jesus' birth in this humble place was part of God's plan to show his love for us. God wanted to show that right from the start of his Son's life on earth, he was truly one of us. Jesus would show that God cares for all of his people, especially the poor and the forgotten. The mystery that the Son of God took on a human nature, or became man, is called the **Incarnation**.

Faith Word

Incarnation the mystery that the Son of God took on a human nature

Activity

Jesus was human as well as God. Fill in the diagram with the things you do, the things Jesus might have done when he was your age, and the things you both do. Write the words in the correct sections of the diagram.

What is the biggest difference between what you do and what Jesus might have done when he was young?

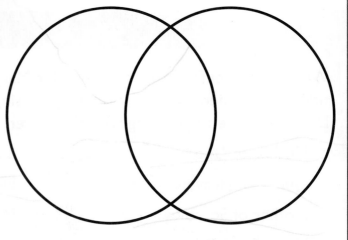

Jesus died on the Cross to save us from sin.

From the beginning of Jesus' earthly life to his Death on the Cross, Jesus is the Son of God. He was born in the same way we are born. Jesus also died on the Cross. Because he was truly human, Jesus' pain and suffering were real. He suffered and died for us because he loves us so much.

The night before his suffering and Death, Jesus shared one last meal with his disciples. He told them, "No one has greater love than this, to lay down one's life for one's friends" (John 15:13).

Jesus did exactly what he told his disciples. He freely laid down his life for them and all people. Jesus sacrificed his life on the Cross.

After Jesus died, he was placed in a tomb. Three days later, his disciples discovered some amazing news. Jesus had risen from the dead! He was alive! Although the disciples did not fully understand what had happened, we know what this news meant. Jesus, the Son of God, suffered, died, and rose from the dead to save us from our sins. He did these things for us so that we can live forever with God in heaven.

The Church shares in the sacrifice of Jesus on the Cross every time we gather at Mass. Through the Mass, we share in the saving grace of Jesus' Death and Resurrection. We celebrate and remember Jesus' sacrifice and his love for us in the Eucharist, the Body and Blood of Christ. In the Eucharist, Jesus is truly present with us and in us.

Jesus Christ ascended to heaven and will come again at the end of time.

After Jesus rose to new life, he came to his disciples many times. He walked, talked, and even ate with them. At first, the disciples did not recognize Jesus. He showed them the wounds in his hands and feet from the Cross. He showed them that he was Jesus, fully alive in a whole new way, never to die again. One day, Jesus led his friends to the top of a hill. There he was taken up from their sight to heaven, where he lives with his Father for all time.

The Bible tells us what happened to the disciples next, while they were looking at the sky:

"Suddenly two men dressed in white garments stood beside them. They said, 'Men of Galilee, why are you standing there looking at the sky? This Jesus who has been taken up from you into heaven will return in the same way as you have seen him going into heaven.'" (Acts of the Apostles 1:10–11)

☑ Show What You Know

Use the words in the Word Bank to complete the sentences.

Holy Spirit   Cross   Holy Family   Incarnation   Blessed Virgin

1. The _____ is the mystery that Jesus, the Son of God, took on a human nature.

2. Jesus, Mary, and Joseph are called the _____ .

3. We name Mary the _____ to honor her obedience to God and commitment to his plan for her.

4. Jesus died on the _____ and rose from the dead so that we can live forever with God in heaven.

5. The _____ filled Mary with grace to be the Mother of God's Son.

Partners in Faith

Saint Joseph

The Holy Spirit told Saint Joseph to marry Mary. Joseph took care of Jesus when he was a boy. He taught Jesus how to be a carpenter. When we need help with our work, we can ask Saint Joseph for help.

 Learn more about the life of Saint Joseph.

Copyright © by William H. Sadlier, Inc. All rights reserved.

Mini-Task

In this lesson, you have learned a lot about Jesus Christ.
You have learned that Jesus Christ is alive with us now and forever.

Imagine you are a reporter. Choose a partner to interview.
Your main question will be: How is Jesus Christ with us today?

Write down two additional questions you would like to ask.
Share your questions with your partner.

Share your interview with the group.

How is Jesus Christ with us today?

 Want to do more? Go to your Portfolio to continue this activity.

 **At Home**

As a family, take a few minutes before or after Mass to look at the crucifix above the altar or at a crucifix in your home.
What details do you notice?

Copyright © by William H. Sadlier, Inc. All rights reserved.

What is the Church?

"I am the vine, you are the branches" (John 15:5). Jesus spoke these words to describe the Church. He is telling us that he is one with all who are baptized.

Saint Peter said that the Church is God's people. Another apostle, Saint Paul, explained that the Church is the Body of Christ on earth. In both the Apostles' Creed and the Nicene Creed, we state what we believe the Church is. We say "I believe in one, holy, catholic, and apostolic Church."

Go to the digital portal for a prayer of intercession.

"For in one Spirit we were all baptized into one body."   1 Corinthians 12:13

Christ is the Head of his Body, the Church.

What do you think of when you hear the word *church*? Do you think of your parish church building? The Church is more than a building. The Church is really made of people.

Saint Peter told us that the Church is the People of God. The Holy Spirit gathers the members of the Church together for worship. All the people we see at Mass belong to the Church. These people include the priest, deacons, lectors, ministers, altar servers, and the assembly of worshipers. Yet the Church also includes people we do not see. The Church is all of God's people who are baptized. The Church includes people who have died, both the souls in Purgatory and those who are in heaven with God.

The Sacrament of Baptism makes us members of the Church. After his Ascension, Jesus called Saint Paul be an apostle. Saint Paul taught that the Church is the Body of Christ. The Church is Christ's Body on earth. Jesus Christ is the Head of the Church.

Who are some people I love who are with God in heaven now?

Did You Know?

Art celebrates the People of God.

Jesus is with us in the Church.

Jesus once said to his followers, "I am the living bread that came down from heaven; whoever eats this bread will live forever" (John 6:51).

Some of the people who heard this could not believe it. How could a person be bread? But Jesus is the Son of God. He is the Bread of Life. This means we can have life with him both now and forever.

We receive the Body and Blood of Christ in Holy Communion. This strengthens us to live as Jesus' disciples every day. It makes us closer to Jesus. The Holy Spirit guides us by helping us to follow Jesus.

Christ is present in the Church and united to her members. By taking part in the sacraments, we are united to Christ and to one another.

Activity

We join the Church when we are baptized. Fill in the following chart. Ask your parents for answers if you don't know them. Tell God you are thankful for your Baptism.

Date you were baptized	
Church where you were baptized	
Your godparents' names	
Saint name (if you have one)	

The Church is one, holy, catholic, and apostolic.

When we pray the Creed at Mass, we use four very important words to describe the Church. We call these descriptions the marks of the Church. We say them in the Creed when we profess our faith.

Faith Words

one a word that describes the Church as being the only Church that Jesus Christ founded

holy growing in God's love and sharing it

catholic universal; open to all people

apostolic a word describing how the Church is founded on the Apostles and passes down their teachings

The Church is one.	The Church is one because her source is one: the Blessed Trinity. The Church is also one because she is the one Body of Christ. The Church is called together by God. Through the Church, God strengthens us to live, love, and worship together.
The Church is holy.	The Church is holy because Christ is holy. God shares his holiness with the Church.
The Church is catholic.	The word catholic means "universal." The Church is catholic because Christ is present with her. The Church is open to all people all over the world. The Church is universal.
The Church is apostolic.	Apostolic comes from the word apostle. Jesus chose the Apostles to be the first leaders of the Church. The Church continues to be led by those who succeeded, or came after, the Apostles: the pope and bishops.

Activity

The marks of the Church are one, holy, catholic, and apostolic.
Match the word to the symbol. Write why each mark is important.

one	holy	catholic	apostolic

The pope and bishops are the successors of the Apostles.

One of the marks of the Church is that the Church is apostolic. Jesus knew that his Church would need a leader. He chose Simon, one of the Apostles, to be that leader. As a sign of his leadership, Jesus changed Simon's name to Peter, which means "rock." Jesus said, "You are Peter, and upon this rock I will build my church" (Matthew 16:18).

At Pentecost, the Apostles began the mission that the Risen Christ gave them. After Jesus' Ascension, Peter and the other Apostles went out to cities and towns, sharing the Good News and baptizing people. They led communities of believers. When it was time, the Apostles chose new leaders to succeed them, just as Jesus had done. A successor is someone who follows or takes the place of another.

The Holy Spirit gave these leaders the same authority that Jesus had given the Apostles. The Apostles' successors have continued to this day. They are called bishops. Bishops are chosen to lead a group of members of the Church.

Bishops are chosen by the pope. Bishops continue the work of the Apostles. They govern, teach, and sanctify the faithful. They do this through prayer, preaching, and celebrating the sacraments. Bishops lead large communities of the Church called dioceses.

Bishops, priests, and deacons are leaders of the Church. The pope is the Bishop of Rome. He is the successor of Saint Peter and the leader of the whole Church. Together with the bishops, the pope leads and guides the entire Church. Priests work with bishops. Deacons work with the bishops and priests to help the whole Church.

Priests preach the message of Jesus and help us to live our faith. They lead in the celebration of the Mass. Priests also continue Jesus' work of forgiving sins and healing in the Sacraments of Penance and Reconciliation and Anointing of the Sick. Deacons help bishops and priests in many ways. But they cannot do everything bishops and priests do. Permanent deacons are single or married men who have special ministries such as preaching, baptizing, or serving the poor.

Faith Words

one   holy   catholic   apostolic

 ## Show What You Know

Match each mark of the Church with its description.

1. one

2. holy

3. catholic

4. apostolic

The Church is holy because Christ is holy.

The Church is founded on the Apostles and passes down their teachings.

The Church acknowledges one Lord, professes one faith, and celebrates one Baptism.

The Church is universal and open to all people all over the world.

Complete the sentence.

5. The pope and _____ are the successors of the Apostles.

Partners in Faith

Saint Nicholas

Saint Nicholas was a rich man who gave away his money to the poor. Nicholas became a priest and then a bishop. He was known for his love of children and protection of sailors.

 Learn more about the life of Saint Nicholas.

Copyright © by William H. Sadlier, Inc. All rights reserved.

Mini-Task

The words of our faith are powerful tools that help us tell others about God's love. Being able to use faith words helps us spread the Good News about God and Jesus Christ.

Review the meaning of the marks of the Church that you have learned in this lesson:

- one
- holy
- catholic
- apostolic

Choose one of the words and draw a way to define it, using only images. Can a partner guess the faith word you illustrated?

 Want to do more? Go to your Portfolio to continue this activity.

 At Home

The word *catholic* means "universal." Talk about other Catholic churches you may have visited. What was the same as or different from your home church?

Copyright © by William H. Sadlier, Inc. All rights reserved.

Unit 2
The Faith Celebrated

The Prodigal Son

Unit Prayer

Leader: Venerable Pierre Toussaint showed God's love through his generous care of orphans and those who were sick. If our hearts are open to the needs of those around us, we will be able to celebrate God's love for us by being like Christ.

Let us listen to how we follow the way of love in the stories of missionary discipleship today.

Leader: Let us pray: Jesus, help us to show the world how much you love us. Give us the courage to be your light in a darkened world, and help all to celebrate your beautiful gift of love. We pray:

Reader: Help us to celebrate your love each day.

All: We will live as the light of Christ.

Reader: Show us how to love each other.

All: We will live as the light of Christ.

Reader: Lift us up when we turn away from your love.

All: We will live as the light of Christ.

Reader: Teach us to love everyone as you love us.

All: We will live as the light of Christ.

Leader: Our Baptism sends us forth to be the light of Christ. Help us to bring God's love to all we meet.

All: Help us to bring God's love to all we meet.

End the Unit Prayer by singing the unit song.

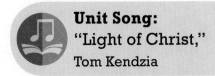
Unit Song:
"Light of Christ,"
Tom Kendzia

Missionary Discipleship

How have we helped others celebrate God's love for us? Do you remember a certain time when this happened? What did you do? How did it make you feel? How did it help you know more about God's love for you?

How does God share his life with us?

God's life of joy and holiness is forever! It is there for each one of us. Jesus wants us to have this life so much that he has given his own life for us. He gave us the sacraments to share his grace with us. Through the celebration of each sacrament, Jesus gives us a special grace of that sacrament.

Go to the digital portal for a prayer of meditation.

"For where two or three are gathered together in my name, there am I in the midst of them."

Matthew 18:20

In the liturgy, the Church participates in Jesus' saving work.

Faith Word

liturgy the Church's participation in the saving work of Jesus Christ

When good things happen to us, we want to share our joy. We might celebrate with family and friends. But how can we celebrate something as important as the eternal life of joy and holiness that God promises us? How can we begin to thank God for sending his only Son, Jesus, to save us?

We celebrate with the Risen Jesus himself. We do this in the **liturgy**. The liturgy is the Church's participation in the saving work of Jesus Christ. The sacraments are the main celebrations of the Church's liturgy. Since the Church is Christ's Body, whenever we gather in the celebration of the Eucharistic liturgy, or Mass, we gather as one in Christ's Body.

When we celebrate Mass, we are led by Jesus, who is the head of his Body, the Church. We are in communion with everyone in the Church. That includes Mary, the Mother of God, the angels, the saints in heaven, the souls in Purgatory, and all of Jesus' Church on earth. Imagine a celebration like this! The Mass is the most special celebration of God's love. It is a celebration with God's whole family!

How do I feel knowing that Jesus is with me?

Did You Know?

At every moment, everywhere in the world, people are joining in the liturgy.

Jesus and the Holy Spirit prepare us to receive grace.

The Holy Spirit prepares us to celebrate the liturgy. When you are at Mass, watch and listen carefully to see how we ask for the Holy Spirit's help.

When we come together at Mass, we join together in praying the Sign of the Cross. The priest welcomes and greets us. He prays that the Holy Spirit will be with us.

During the Mass, we hear about God's love from the Old Testament and the New Testament. God is the author of Sacred Scripture. The Holy Spirit inspired human beings who lived in different times and places to write down the books of Sacred Scripture. When we listen to the readings at Mass, we hear the Word of God. We receive God's grace through the Holy Spirit. We are strengthened in our faith so that we can receive Christ in the Eucharist.

During the Liturgy of the Eucharist, the priest extends his hands over the bread and wine. He prays aloud, asking God to send the Holy Spirit so that the bread and wine may become the Body and Blood of Christ. The priest prays for all those present to be filled with the Holy Spirit.

Jesus gave the Church the sacraments.

Have you ever wanted to see Jesus face-to-face? What would it be like to hear him speak to you? How would you feel if Jesus held your hand or gave you a hug?

During Jesus' time on earth, many people wanted to see and touch him. One woman had been suffering from a bleeding sickness for twelve years. She wanted Jesus to heal her, but the crowd around Jesus was very large.

"[She] came up behind him and touched the tassel on his cloak. She said to herself, 'If only I can touch his cloak, I shall be cured.' Jesus turned around and saw her, and said, 'Courage, daughter! Your faith has saved you.' And from that hour the woman was cured" (Matthew 9:20–22).

In this Gospel passage, Jesus' cloak was an *extension* of his power to heal. The woman had great faith in Jesus' healing and saving power. Jesus knows that we need to see, touch, and hear signs of his presence among us. He has given the Church the **sacraments**. We call the sacraments effective signs because we truly receive God's grace through their symbols and rites. Each sacrament grants us a particular grace to make us holy.

Faith Word

sacraments special signs given to us by Jesus through which we receive God's grace

The Church celebrates seven sacraments. They are Baptism, Confirmation, Eucharist, Penance and Reconciliation, Anointing of the Sick, Holy Orders, and Matrimony.

The sacraments are part of the Church's liturgy. They are the instruments of the Holy Spirit at work in Jesus' Body, the Church.

In the Gospel, Jesus shows us another important truth. Even though the crowd around him was great, Jesus was aware of the needs of one single person. In the sacraments, Jesus is present to us personally. For example, in the Sacrament of Baptism, it is Christ who baptizes us. In the Sacrament of Penance and Reconciliation, it is Christ who forgives us. Through the sacraments, each of us has a share in the eternal life Jesus promises.

Activity

Fill out the chart with what you know about some of the Church's sacraments. Put a check mark next to the sacraments you have celebrated. Compare your chart with a friend's.

Sacrament	Who receives it	I have celebrated this sacrament	What I know about this sacrament
Baptism			
Eucharist			
Reconciliation			

Sacramentals prepare us to receive God's grace.

A **sacramental** is something that opens us to receive God's grace in the sacraments. Sacramentals help us make our lives holy and act on God's grace given in the sacraments. Holy water is an example of a sacramental. It has been blessed by a priest or deacon. We bless ourselves by making the Sign of the Cross with holy water when we enter the church. This reminds us of the water of the Sacrament of Baptism that cleanses us from sin. It reminds us that we are blessed by God through Jesus and his Cross. If we are going to church to receive the sacraments, blessing ourselves with holy water can prepare us for the grace we are about to receive.

Sacramentals can be objects like statues, medals, rosaries, holy candles, or crucifixes. They can be blessings of people, places, and food. Actions, such as making the Sign of the Cross or genuflecting, are sacramentals.

Faith Word

sacramentals
blessings of people, actions, and religious objects that help us grow in faith and act on God's grace given in the sacraments

Activity

Sacramentals can be objects, actions, or blessings. Fill in the blanks to write your own blessing. Use it to bless a friend.

Dear God,

Bless my friend _____.

Keep him/her _____.

Help us both to always _____.

Amen.

Faith Words

liturgy   sacraments   sacramentals

 Show What You Know

Circle the correct answer.

1. _____ are special signs given to us by Jesus through which we receive God's grace.

   Sacraments | Sacramentals

2. The participation of the Church in the saving work of Jesus Christ is called the _____.

   liturgy | sacraments

3. _____ are blessings, actions, and objects that help us grow in faith and act on God's grace given in the sacraments.

   Sacramentals | Celebrations

Write the answer to the question.

4. How many sacraments does the Church celebrate?

   _____

Partners in Faith

Saint Dominic Savio

Saint Dominic Savio loved the Eucharist. He said the day of his first Communion was the happiest day of his life. At school, he was known as a peacemaker who always looked after those in need. He started a club in honor of the Virgin Mary. He helped many people grow in their love for God.

 Learn more about the life of Saint Dominic Savio.

Copyright © by William H. Sadlier, Inc. All rights reserved.

How can I share God's love and joy with others?

Mini-Task

List some ways that you can show God's love to others.

Imagine that you work for a local video company. You have been asked to produce a ninety-second commercial that will inspire viewers to share God's love and joy with others.

Choose a style for your video: interview, animation, music video, or short story with a cast of characters.

Outline your video in the storyboard.

 Want to do more? Go to your Portfolio to continue this activity.

With your family, read or remember a Gospel passage in which Jesus heals, forgives, or gives nourishment. Talk about how Jesus heals, forgives, and feeds you in the sacraments.

Copyright © by William H. Sadlier, Inc. All rights reserved.

How do we praise and thank God?

Praising and thanking God is something we can do every day. We do not have to pray the same way every day. The liturgical year is the Church's calendar of feast days and celebrations. It helps us recall and celebrate all that Jesus did for our salvation.

Go to the digital portal for a prayer of thanksgiving.

"God blessed the seventh day and made it holy, because on it he rested from all the work he had done in creation."

Genesis 2:3

The Church celebrates Jesus' life and saving work all year long.

The Scripture readings we hear at Mass in the Liturgy of the Word follow a certain order. The Church's calendar guides the readings. We call the Church's calendar of feasts and celebrations the **liturgical year**.

The liturgical year begins with the season of Advent, when we prepare for the birth of Jesus. During the season of Advent, we remember John the Baptist. John told people to get ready for the coming Messiah. At Christmas and in January, we remember Jesus' birth and his early life. During the season of Easter, we remember Jesus' Resurrection and Ascension. We remember the coming of the Holy Spirit at Pentecost. During the season of Ordinary Time, we hear about Jesus' parables and healings.

Each year, as we listen to the Scripture readings, the Holy Spirit guides us to learn something new about God, our faith, and ourselves.

Faith Word

liturgical year the celebration throughout the year of the mysteries of Jesus' birth, life, Death, and Resurrection

Activity

Special colors are used for each of the seasons of the liturgical year. Read what the colors stand for and then match the color to the season or feast.

1. Purple: sorrow and waiting   Lent

2. Green: learning about and   Christmas
   following Jesus
                                                 Pentecost
3. White or Gold: joy
                                                 Ordinary Time
4. Red: Holy Spirit

How can you use this season's color to help you remember what the Church does during the season? Trade ideas with a partner.

All around the world, Catholics use their local customs to praise and worship God.

No matter where you are in the world, you can worship God in the Mass. At some Catholic churches, the Mass might include symbols from the local culture. The Mass is also usually prayed in the local language. But it is always the same Mass celebrated by the whole Church.

Devotions draw us closer to God.

We praise and worship God in the liturgy. We also praise God through other forms of prayer, too. We can do this in small ways, at home, at school, and even when we are traveling or playing with friends. **Devotions** help us pray and show our love for God.

Devotions include prayers we say with our families, such as the Rosary. During the season of Lent, we pray the Stations of the Cross. We might take a trip to visit a shrine or another holy place. This is called a pilgrimage. We might take part in a procession, where we walk and pray together. All of these devotions can help us grow in faith.

We can also remember that God has given us Mary and the saints to show us how to live. When we honor them, we show that we want to follow Jesus the same way they did. There are many celebrations of Mary and the saints throughout the year. There might be statues or pictures of Mary and the saints in and around your church or in your home. Their images and feast days are reminders of how to live a holy life. Devotions to Mary and the saints are ways for us to get closer to Christ every day of our lives.

Faith Words

Liturgy of the Word   **liturgical year**
devotions

 Show What You Know

Match the terms to the correct definitions.

1. devotions

2. liturgical year

3. Liturgy of
the Word

the many traditions, outside of the liturgy, that help us pray and show our love for God

the part of the Mass when we listen and respond to God's Word

the celebration throughout the year of the mysteries of Jesus' birth, life, Death, and Resurrection

Partners in Faith

Saint Gregory the Great

Saint Gregory the Great was pope from 590 to 604. He helped develop the Mass as we know it. The people loved Pope Gregory because he cared for the poor. A special kind of music called Gregorian chant is named after him.

 Learn more about the life of Saint Gregory the Great.

Copyright © by William H. Sadlier, Inc. All rights reserved.

Mini-Task

Preparing to hear God's Word helps us understand what God is saying in the readings at Mass.

Learn more about the readings that will be part of this coming Sunday's Mass.

Write the book, chapter, and verses of the reading in the left column. Read each passage with a partner.

A takeaway is a key fact or idea that you will remember at Mass on Sunday. What is a takeaway from each reading? Write it in the right column.

Date:	Takeaway
First Reading:	
Responsorial Psalm:	
Second Reading:	
Gospel Reading:	

 Want to do more? Go to your Portfolio to continue this activity.

 **At Home**

What times are Masses celebrated in your parish? Look at the church bulletin or parish Web site to find the times. What time does your family go to Mass?

Copyright © by William H. Sadlier, Inc. All rights reserved.

How do we become members of the Church?

In the Sacraments of Christian Initiation, Jesus calls, welcomes, and strengthens us to be members of his Church. The Holy Spirit places a spiritual character on our souls that cannot be removed. This mark means that we belong to God forever. We are marked as Jesus' witnesses. In the Eucharist, we receive the Body of Christ. We receive strength and nourishment to live as Jesus' disciples.

Go to the digital portal for a prayer of thanksgiving.

"When we receive [the Eucharist], our hearts are overcome with the certainty of Jesus' love."

Homily of Pope Francis, Solemnity of the Most Holy Body and Blood of Christ, 2017

The Sacraments of Christian Initiation welcome us into the Church.

Can you remember a time when you began something new? Maybe you moved to a new neighborhood or joined a new sports team. At times like these, signs of welcome can help us. Small signs, like a smile or being invited to play, can make us feel at home.

Jesus welcomes us into the Church with sacred signs called the **Sacraments of Christian Initiation**. The word *initiation* is another way of saying "beginning." These sacraments are Baptism, Confirmation, and Eucharist.

Faith Word

Sacraments of Christian Initiation
the Sacraments of Baptism, Confirmation, and Eucharist, which make us part of the Church

The Sacraments of Christian Initiation	
Baptism	This sacrament cleanses us of Original Sin and forgives any sins we have committed. We are welcomed into the Church and called to be disciples.
Confirmation	This sacrament strengthens our Baptism. We are sealed with the Gift of the Holy Spirit.
Eucharist	In this sacrament, we receive Jesus' Body and Blood in Holy Communion. Receiving Holy Communion unites us more closely to Jesus and all the members of the Church.

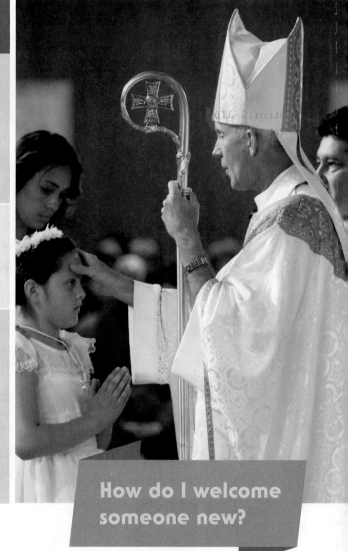

How do I welcome someone new?

Did You Know?

 The early Christians baptized by immersion.

In Baptism we are born to new life in Christ.

"What's your name?" When you meet someone, this is the first question you might ask. It is the same kind of question the priest or deacon asks the parents and godparents of a baby being baptized in the Church.

God already knows our name. But in **Baptism**, Jesus calls us by name to become part of his Church, the Body of Christ. The minister of Baptism traces a cross on the forehead of the one to be baptized, saying, "I claim you for Christ our Savior by the sign of his cross." He invites parents and godparents to do the same thing. This is a reminder that the Cross and Jesus' life, Death, and Resurrection all guide us every day of our lives.

Baptism is the first sacrament we receive. In Baptism, a spiritual character, or seal, is placed on our souls. This character is from the Holy Spirit, and it lasts forever. It consecrates us. That means we belong to Christ forever. This is why we are baptized only once. The Sacrament of Baptism gives us new life in Christ. Through Baptism, God frees us from Original Sin. He forgives any sins we may have committed. God gives us his gift of grace, adopts us as sons and daughters, unites us to the Church, and recreates us to respond to God's life of grace.

Faith Word

Baptism the sacrament in which we become members of the Church

Activity

Jesus calls each of us by name in a special way at our Baptism.

Write your whole name: _____

Trace a cross with your finger and say, "I know that Jesus has

called me, _____, to be

a member of his Church in Baptism."

Make a Sign of the Cross on a friend's forehead. Using that person's

whole name, say: "_____, Jesus

has called you to be a member of his Church in Baptism."

Confirmation completes our Baptism.

The grace we receive in our Baptism is deepened in the **Sacrament of Confirmation**. Confirmation unites us more closely to Christ. We receive the special strength of the Holy Spirit to be true witnesses of Jesus Christ.

Like Baptism, Confirmation places a special character on our souls. This mark lasts forever. That is why we receive this sacrament only once. When we receive the Sacrament of Confirmation, the bishop traces the Sign of the Cross with Sacred Chrism on the forehead of the person receiving Confirmation. As he does this, he says the name of the person and these words:

Be sealed with the Gift of the Holy Spirit.
—Order of Confirmation, 27

In the Roman Catholic Church, most people receive the Sacrament of Confirmation between the ages of 7 and 16. In other Catholic Churches, people receive the Sacrament of Confirmation immediately after their Baptism.

Faith Word

Confirmation the sacrament in which we are sealed with the Gift of the Holy Spirit

The Eucharist is the heart of the Church's life.

The night before he died, Jesus celebrated the feast of Passover with his friends. This is a special meal of thanksgiving to God for freeing the Jewish people from their slavery in Egypt. The Jewish people remember that God protected them from the angel of death that "passed over" their houses. God protected his people from the suffering that came to Egypt. Jesus celebrated the Passover meal in a new way with his disciples. We call this meal the Last Supper.

Faith Word

Eucharist the sacrament of Jesus' Body and Blood

"While they were eating, Jesus took bread, said the blessing, broke it, and giving it to his disciples said, 'Take and eat; this is my body.' Then he took a cup, gave thanks, and gave it to them, saying, 'Drink from it, all of you, for this is my blood of the covenant, which will be shed on behalf of many for the forgiveness of sins'" (Matthew 26:26–28).

At the Last Supper, Jesus gave us the **Sacrament of the Eucharist**. The Eucharist is the sacrament of Jesus' own Body and Blood. At each celebration of the Eucharist, the Church follows Jesus' command at the Last Supper: "Do this in memory of me" (Luke 22:19).

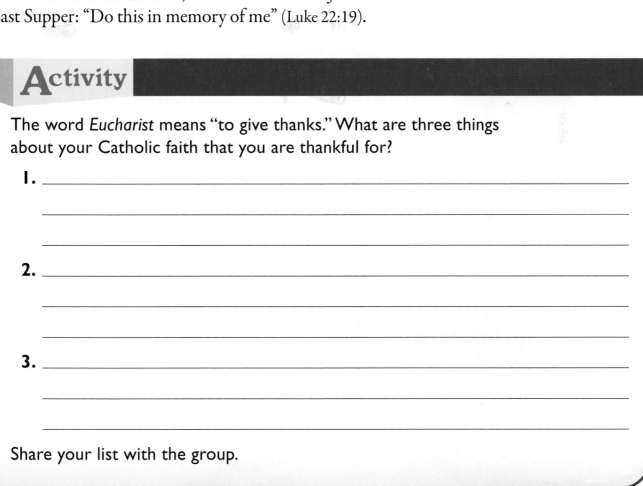

Activity

The word *Eucharist* means "to give thanks." What are three things about your Catholic faith that you are thankful for?

1. _____

_____

_____

2. _____

_____

_____

3. _____

_____

_____

Share your list with the group.

What does it mean to me that I am a member of the Church?

Mini-Task

We are each members of groups. For example, we belong at least to a family and to this class. Think of three groups that you are part of, and write how you joined each group.

In the space below, write how becoming part of the Church is the same as or different from a way that you joined one of the other groups.

Group 1
_____

How I joined:
_____

Group 2
_____

How I joined:
_____

Group 3
_____

How I joined:
_____

Christian Initiation	
How we join the Church:	
Similarities:	**Differences:**
1.	1.
2.	2.
3.	3.

 Want to do more? Go to your Portfolio to continue this activity.

 At Home

When you go to Mass, what are the things you see and hear in the church that help you to feel close to Jesus and listen to him? Talk about this with your family.

Copyright © by William H. Sadlier, Inc. All rights reserved.

Jesus healed the sick and forgave sinners. He told stories to give us examples of the greatness of God's love and forgiveness. But Jesus' healing, forgiveness, and stories were not just for the people of his time. Jesus gave his Church the power to heal and forgive in his name. Through the Sacraments of Healing, all of us can receive God's saving grace, healing, and forgiveness. The Sacraments of Healing are the Sacraments of Penance and Reconciliation and Anointing of the Sick.

Go to the digital portal for a *Lectio* and *Visio Divina* prayer.

"Rejoice with me because I have found my lost sheep." Luke 15:6

We celebrate Jesus' forgiveness and healing in the Church today.

One day, Jesus was teaching a large crowd of people. They had come from nearby villages and were gathered inside a house to hear Jesus speak.

"And some men brought on a stretcher a man who was paralyzed. . . . But not finding a way to bring him in because of the crowd, they went up on the roof and lowered him on the stretcher through the tiles into the middle in front of Jesus. When he saw their faith, he said, 'As for you, your sins are forgiven. . . . But that you may know that the Son of Man has authority on earth to forgive sins'— he said to the man who was paralyzed, 'I say to you, rise, pick up your stretcher, and go home.' He stood up immediately before them, picked up what he had been lying on, and went home, glorifying God. Then astonishment seized them all and they glorified God, and, struck with awe, they said, 'We have seen incredible things today'" (Luke 5:18–20, 24–26).

Today, we can say that we have seen incredible things, too. Through the power of the Holy Spirit, the Church continues the healing work of Jesus. The Church does this through the Sacraments of Healing. They are Penance and Reconciliation and Anointing of the Sick.

Faith Words

Penance and Reconciliation the sacrament in which God is with us, forgiving our sins

How do I feel when I need forgiveness or healing?

Did You Know?

 Today, Jesus continues to heal through the Church.

In the **Sacrament of Penance and Reconciliation**, we are forgiven in the name of the Father, and of the Son, and of the Holy Spirit. We receive God's forgiveness for sins we have committed. We receive *absolution*. This means we are forgiven through the words and actions of the priest, who acts on Christ's behalf.

In this sacrament, we do three things:

• We express sorrow for our sins. This is called *contrition*, or *repentance*.

• We tell our sins to a priest. This is called *confession*. The priest may talk to us about ways we can love God and others better.

• We show that we are willing to do better. The priest gives us a *penance*. This is a prayer or action we do after we receive absolution. Accepting penance shows we are willing to heal any harm we have done by sinning.

Activity

When we receive the Sacrament of Penance and Reconciliation, we say we are sorry for our sins. What are some reasons that someone would be sorry for his or her sins? Write down one or two reasons.

_____

_____

_____

We ask forgiveness in Jesus' name.

Jesus told a story to show how God forgives us. It was about a son who asked his father to give him all the wealth that was coming to him. After his father gave him the money, the son left home. The son spent all the money. He was hungry, and he started working, taking care of a farmer's pigs. The son was very sad. He decided to go back home to his father.

"While he was still a long way off, his father caught sight of him, and was filled with compassion. He ran to his son, embraced him and kissed him. His son said to him, 'Father, I have sinned against heaven and against you; I no longer deserve to be called your son.' But his father ordered his servants, 'Quickly bring the finest robe and put it on him; put a ring on his finger and sandals on his feet. . . . Then let us celebrate with a feast, because this son of mine was dead, and has come to life again; he was lost, and has been found.' Then the celebration began." (Luke 15:20–24)

The father's love for his son tells us about God's love for us. When even one sinner asks God's forgiveness in Jesus' name, the whole Body of Christ is made stronger. We all share in the joy of God's forgiveness and love.

Activity

Imagine that you are the prodigal son in the Scripture story. Have a friend pretend to be the father in the story. Tell your friend how you feel when you see the father. Have your friend tell how he or she feels when seeing the son. Trade places.

Talk with your friend about whether it is easier to ask for forgiveness or to forgive.

In the Sacrament of Penance, the Church forgives us in Jesus' name.

Our Baptism makes us members of the Church, the Body of Christ. Saint Paul tells us that "if [one] part suffers, all the parts suffer with it; if one part is honored, all the parts share its joy" (1 Corinthians 12:26). As the Body of Christ, we all hurt when any member of the Body of Christ sins. Sin not only hurts God and others, but it also weakens the whole Church.

The Sacrament of Penance and Reconciliation is the Church's celebration of God's love and mercy. It brings us back into God's grace and friendship. It makes us and the whole Church stronger.

We receive forgiveness and peace in Jesus' name. We hear this in the words of the priest:

"God, the Father of mercies, through the death and resurrection of his Son has reconciled the world to himself and sent the Holy Spirit among us for the forgiveness of sins; through the ministry of the Church may God give you pardon and peace, and I absolve you from your sins in the name of the Father, and of the Son, and of the Holy Spirit."

—Rite of Penance, 46

All members of the Church share in Christ's mission.

In the Old Testament, priests, prophets, and kings were anointed with oil. This anointing was a sign that God had given them a special mission. In the Sacraments of Baptism and Confirmation, we are anointed with holy oil called *chrism*. This is a sign that we have been given a mission as Christ's followers. We share in Christ's mission.

Does this mean that all the members of the Church share in the work of Jesus? Yes, but we do not all share in Jesus' work in the exact same way. We use the term **common priesthood of the faithful** to describe how all baptized people share in the work of Jesus. This means we share in Christ's mission of sacrifice and service to others. We are strengthened in our mission by the Holy Spirit in the sacraments.

The **Sacraments at the Service of Communion** give special graces to some members of the Church to help the whole Church do the work of Jesus. These sacraments are Holy Orders and Matrimony.

Faith Words

common priesthood of the faithful
Christ's priestly mission, shared by all who are baptized

Sacraments at the Service of Communion
sacraments that strengthen people to serve God and the Church through the vocations of Matrimony or Holy Orders

How do I share in Jesus' mission of love and service to God and his people?

Did You Know?

Every person is unique.

Bishops, priests, and deacons teach and guide the Church.

After Jesus' Resurrection and Ascension, the Apostles went out spreading the Good News. They built small communities of believers. They chose leaders and ministers in each community.

The Apostles laid their hands on those chosen in Jesus' name. This was a sign of God's grace. We name these leaders bishops. Others were chosen to work with the Apostles as their co-workers, and the Bible names these co-workers priests. The Apostles chose a third group of men to help the bishops and priests. The Bible names these helpers deacons. Some of these leaders continued the Apostles' ministry. They also went out and spread the Good News of Jesus.

This direct line of leadership, service, and ministry has continued from the Apostles all the way to today. Some men are called to serve Jesus as ordained ministers in the Church. In the **Sacrament of Holy Orders**, they are ordained as bishops, priests, and deacons. In this sacrament, a bishop prays and lays hands on a man who is being ordained, just as the Apostles did. These men are consecrated for a particular service in the Church. They receive special graces to carry out the Church's ministry.

Faith Word

Holy Orders the sacrament in which baptized men are ordained to serve the Church as bishops, priests, or deacons

Activity

Write one thing each person does to share in Christ's mission of sacrifice and service in the Church.

My parent _____.

My catechist _____.

My priest _____.

Now write one thing you can do to share in Christ's mission.

_____

Bishops, priests, and deacons are all essential to the Church.

Bishops usually lead and care for large communities called dioceses. A diocese is made up of parishes, schools, colleges, and even hospitals. The Bishop of Rome is the pope. He follows an unbroken line of leaders that goes back to Saint Peter. The pope has a special responsibility to care for and lead the whole Church, all over the world. Bishops are called to work with the pope to watch over all those in their care, especially people in need.

Priests are celibate ordained men who preach the message of Jesus and help us live our faith. Priests lead us in the celebration of the Mass and the sacraments. In the Roman Catholic Church, priests promise not to marry. This is a sign that they want to give their whole life to the family of God, in service to the Church.

Every priest is a **deacon** first. Some men are called to be permanent deacons. This means that after they become deacons, they serve as deacons for the rest of their lives. Permanent deacons can be single or married men. Deacons are ordained to help bishops and priests. But they cannot do everything bishops and priests do. Deacons can baptize and assist at the celebration of marriage. They can also preach, assist at Mass, and serve the People of God.

Faith Words

bishops ordained men who serve and lead the Church; bishops are successors of the Apostles

priests ordained ministers who serve the Church by working with bishops to lead, teach, and celebrate the Eucharist and other sacraments

deacons ordained men who serve the Church by helping the bishop and priests

Faith Word

Matrimony the sacrament in which a baptized man and a baptized woman become husband and wife and promise to be faithful to each other for the rest of their lives; also called marriage

Matrimony is a Sacrament at the Service of Communion.

From the very beginning, God has planned for people to get married. In the Old Testament we read: "That is why a man leaves his father and mother and clings to his wife, and the two of them become one body" (Genesis 2:24).

In the New Testament, we see that Jesus celebrated marriage when he attended a wedding feast in Cana (see John 2:1–12). When the married couple ran out of wine to serve their guests, Jesus helped them by turning water into wine. This is the first miracle of Jesus in John's Gospel. The Church has attached great importance to Jesus' presence at the wedding in Cana. His presence shows us the goodness and holy nature of marriage by instituting it as a sacrament.

In the **Sacrament of Matrimony**, a baptized man and baptized woman become husband and wife. God's plan for marriage includes the lifelong unity between one man and one woman, and their willingness to cooperate with God in the procreation of children. The grace of the Sacrament of Matrimony strengthens the couple's unity and their love. This grace also helps the couple welcome children and educate them in the faith. The married man and woman grow in holiness as they serve God and the Church together.

Those who are not married also serve God and the Church. Single people can perform various roles in the liturgy and in their parish. They can act as Christian role models in their community.

We call our family a "church of the home."

Did you know that your family is a church? Whether your family is large or small, you are called as a family to be a domestic church, or "church of the home." Think about what it means to be members of Jesus' Church. We are part of one Body of Christ. We love each other as Jesus loves us. Our families need to help us understand this well.

When we care for our families, we are able to feel Jesus' love. Our families can help us grow in our faith as we pray and worship together. God wants families to learn what it means to be disciples of Jesus who work together, deal with our differences, and learn to be patient with one another.

This is what Jesus wants for us. As churches of the home, our families have a mission to serve, just as the Church does. Family members can go out and share the Good News. They can share God's love with other family members. They can comfort and bring help to those in need. Our whole Church family is called to be a light to the world and a joyful, loving sign of Jesus' grace.

Activity

How is your family a "church of the home"? Write two ways you can love your family more this week.

1. _____

2. _____

Share your ideas with a partner.

Faith Words

common priesthood of the faithful
Sacraments at the Service of Communion
Holy Orders   bishops   priests
deacons   Matrimony

 Show What You Know

Choose the Faith Word that best completes each sentence.

1. The Sacraments at the Service of Communion are

_____ and Matrimony.

2. _____ are men who have received the Sacrament of Holy Orders to serve the Church by helping the bishop and priests.

3. Christ's priestly mission, shared by all who are baptized, is the

_____.

4. The _____ are the successors of the Apostles who lead the Church.

Partners in Faith

Blessed Stanley Rother

Stanley Rother was from Oklahoma. He went to Guatemala as a missionary. He knew if he stayed there, he would be in danger. He would not leave. Blessed Stanley is the first priest and martyr born in the United States to be beatified.

 Learn more about the life of Blessed Stanley Rother.

Copyright © by William H. Sadlier, Inc. All rights reserved.

Mini-Task

Choose one person you know who serves God and the Church.

Design a profile of faith for that person.

PROFILE OF FAITH

Name _____

Description of Vocation _____

_____

Roles _____

_____

_____

_____

_____

_____

What are some ways this person serves God and the Church?

 Want to do more? Go to your Portfolio to continue this activity.

Think about people in your family who have helped you and how they know Jesus in different ways. Try to find time to say "thank you" for the ways they help.

Copyright © by William H. Sadlier, Inc. All rights reserved.

How do we live what we believe?

The Transfiguration of Jesus

God wants us to share in his life and love.

God created us in his own image and likeness. He gives us many gifts. We can see and touch some gifts, like the earth and our families. Other gifts cannot be seen. God gave each of us a body. God also gave each of us a soul, which we cannot see. Our souls especially are in the image of God.

God has given each of us a mind so that we can think about things. We can speak with one another. We can share thoughts and feelings. We can also choose between what is right and wrong. We do not have to do anything to earn these gifts. God gives them to every human person. God does this simply because he loves us.

How do I know God's love?

God has given us the gift of the Church. Through the Church, we receive God's grace, strength, and healing in the sacraments. With all these good gifts, we can share in God's life and love. This is what makes us truly happy. This is God's plan for us and for the whole world.

Did You Know?

 People who use their gifts make a difference.

We are called to care for one another.

God sent Jesus to show us a perfect way to live. Jesus showed us how to love others the way God loves us. At the Last Supper, Jesus poured water into a bowl. Then he washed the disciples' feet. When he had finished, Jesus said:

"Do you realize what I have done for you? You call me 'teacher' and 'master,' and rightly so, for indeed I am. If I, therefore, the master and teacher, have washed your feet, you ought to wash one another's feet. I have given you a model to follow, so that as I have done for you, you should also do" (John 13:12–15).

Activity

God gives us many gifts. Some of them cannot be seen. In each of the boxes, write or draw a gift that God has given you that cannot be seen. It might be a talent, a thought, or a feeling.

Tell a partner how you can use one of these gifts to share God's love with others.

A "model" is an example. Jesus was showing us how his Father wants us to treat others. In Jesus' time, washing a person's feet was a humble action of service.

By washing his disciples' feet, Jesus showed us that he is the servant of all. Jesus serves us because he loves us. We are called to serve others and show them the same love Jesus showed us.

Activity

Jesus wants us to serve others. Write one way you can serve each of these people.

My parents: _____

My siblings: _____

My friends: _____

My neighbors: _____

Pick one way to serve this week. Tell a friend why you want to do it.

God gives us freedom to choose what is good and holy.

Jesus told the disciples he was giving them a model to follow. He was also reminding them of their freedom. The disciples had the freedom to follow or not to follow Jesus' example. God gives each of us this freedom. We can think and make our own choices.

That means no one else makes our choices for us. We take responsibility for our decisions. We own every choice we make. Some choices are easy, like deciding to help out with your family's chores. Some choices are hard, like standing up to a friend or classmate who is breaking an important rule.

Remember, your Baptism made you a member of God's family. You received the grace of the Holy Spirit. The sacraments give you graces and strength to help you make good decisions.

The natural law is written in our hearts.

We are made in God's image. That means God's wisdom and goodness are deep in our hearts. God is always guiding us toward what is good. We call this **natural law**. Natural law is how we know that some actions are good and others are bad. For example, we know that taking something that belongs to someone else is wrong. Natural law is true for all people, at all times, and in all places. It is what helps people create rules and laws to keep all of us safe and happy.

Sometimes we need help understanding natural law. God imprints the natural law on our hearts. Through grace and reason, we are able to apply it to our lives in order to know and choose what is good in specific situations. When we live by following God's natural law, we are doing what God wants for us. This will always make us happy.

Faith Word

natural law God's wisdom, deep in our hearts, that guides us toward what is good

Faith Word

natural law

☑ Show What You Know

Circle the correct answer.

1. Jesus calls us to _____ others.

serve | feed

2. God gives each of us _____ to choose what is good and holy.

friendship | freedom

3. _____ law is God's wisdom, deep in our hearts, that guides us toward what is good.

Natural | Normal

Write the answer to the question.

Who is our model to follow for how God wants us to treat people?

_____

Partners in Faith

Blessed Anne-Marie Javouhey

Blessed Anne-Marie Javouhey cared for all children. At first, she ran a school for poor children in France. Later, her work spread to Africa, South America, and around the world.

 Learn more about the life of Blessed Anne-Marie Javouhey.

Copyright © by William H. Sadlier, Inc. All rights reserved.

Good moral choices help us to live in God's Kingdom.

Do you know what God wants most for you? God wants you to live in communion with him. God has created you for true happiness. Sometimes we think certain people or things will make us happy. But this happiness does not last. The happiness that comes from living in communion with the Blessed Trinity is the true happiness God offers us.

Jesus shows us how we can live in God's grace. He has given us the teachings we call the **Beatitudes**. In the Beatitudes, Jesus shows us how our good choices can make us happy or blessed. This is how we live in God's grace now and forever. These teachings are so important, Jesus wanted everyone to hear. He climbed a mountain to explain. Here is how he began:

"Blessed are the poor in spirit,
    for theirs is the kingdom of
    heaven" (Matthew 5:3).

People who are "poor in spirit" place all their trust in God. They know only God will make them truly happy. They are blessed by God.

Beatitudes

Faith Word

Beatitudes the teachings of Jesus that describe the way to live in God's happiness

> **What kind of choices do I make?**

Did You Know?

 Gratitude can become a habit.

Faith Word

compassion the ability to understand and share in the feelings of another

Each Beatitude shows a way that we can be blessed. That leads to happiness with God forever. For example, Jesus says:

"Blessed are they who mourn,
    for they will be comforted" (Matthew 5:4).

To mourn is to be sad. How can people who mourn be happy? Jesus is saying that when others are suffering or need help, we must act with **compassion**. Compassion is the desire and ability to understand and share in the feelings of another. When we show compassion, we are also showing love.

Here is another Beatitude:

"Blessed are the clean of heart,
    for they will see God" (Matthew 5:8).

To be "clean of heart," we put God first. All of our thoughts, words, and actions are about God's love.

Activity

Each time we make the right choice, we build our conscience. We make it stronger. Fill in the word cloud with ways that you can form your conscience.

prayer
_____

_____   _____

right   CONSCIENCE   help
_____   _____

_____   wrong

_____   _____

How do the Beatitudes help me respond to God's love?

Mini-Task

Create a tree map for one of the Beatitudes.

Review the Beatitudes, and build your tree based on what is most important about your Beatitude. (Add branches to your map if you need to.)

Teach the Beatitude to a partner, using your map.

 Want to do more? Go to your Portfolio to continue this activity.

At Home

Jesus teaches us how to live in the Beatitudes. Find the Beatitudes in Matthew 5:1–12. Have each person in your family choose one Beatitude to live out this week.

Copyright © by William H. Sadlier, Inc. All rights reserved.

Loving others is more than saying "I love you." It means deciding to do good for someone and then *doing it.* God shows us ways to do this. He gave us the Ten Commandments, which is one of the ways God shows us he loves us. He is showing us how to live in his love.

Go to the digital portal for a prayer of meditation.

"So then the law is holy, and the commandment is holy and righteous and good."

Romans 7:12

God's laws are divinely revealed.

In the Old Testament, we read accounts about God's people before Jesus' birth. The Book of Exodus tells how Moses led them out of slavery in Egypt. God's people wandered in the desert for forty years. There, God led Moses up a mountain and gave him the **Ten Commandments**. These are God's laws. They are part of the natural law. They helped God's people know how to love God and love others. This is how God wants us all to live. He wants us to follow his ways so we can live in his Kingdom forever. By giving us the Ten Commandments, God shows his love for us.

God's law is fulfilled in Jesus, who frees us from sin and gives us the grace to follow God's law through his Passion, Death, and Resurrection. In his teachings, Jesus showed us how to fully understand and live the Ten Commandments. He also gave us the Beatitudes, which are promises from God to his faithful people. Each beatitude shows us the blessings in store for those who follow Jesus. God wants us to be happy! Following God's law will make us truly happy, so God sent his Son to gain for us the grace to live out his teachings.

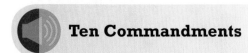

Ten Commandments

Faith Word

Ten Commandments
God's laws that were given to Moses, to help people know how to love God and others

How do laws keep me safe?

Did You Know?

Artists have shown Moses in different ways.

The commandments call us to love God above all else.

God gave his people the Ten Commandments. This made them happy. They knew these laws came from God. That made the commandments holy. By following the commandments, God's people honored him. They worshiped God alone. They set apart one day of the week as a special day to honor God. In the Book of Genesis, we read that God created the heavens and the earth in six days. On the seventh day, he rested:

"God blessed the seventh day and made it holy" (Genesis 2:3).

The seventh day was a day of rest and worship for God's people. It was called the Sabbath.

Like God's people in the Old Testament, we obey the Ten Commandments. We put God first in our lives. We honor God by loving others. We show our love for God by praying to him and worshiping him.

Prayer is listening and talking to God with our minds and hearts. When we pray, we can grow closer to God.

Worship is giving God thanks and praise. We praise God for his goodness. We adore God and thank him for his many gifts. We offer our love to God.

We also set aside a day to rest and worship God. We do this on Sunday, the first day of the week. This is when Jesus rose from the dead. This is why we call Sunday the Lord's Day. Our greatest act of love and worship is the Mass. At Mass, we become one with Jesus, the Son of God. At Mass, we are strengthened by the Eucharist to live as God's people.

For many, the Lord's Day is also a day of rest and relaxation. When we rest, we can become more aware of God's presence in our lives. We can use this day to share the gifts God has given us. We can share a meal with our families. We can care for the needs of others. These are all ways we honor God and keep his day holy.

Faith Words

prayer listening and talking to God

worship giving God thanks and praise

Activity

We pray to God and we worship God, but prayer and worship are not exactly the same. How are prayer and worship alike, and how are they different? Write your thoughts below.

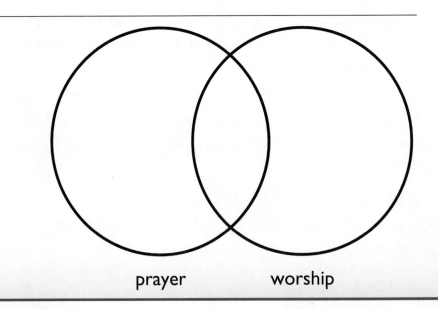

prayer   worship

The commandments call us to love and respect ourselves and others.

The Ten Commandments show us how we should treat others. We should not lie or steal. We should not take another person's life. All of these laws are based on an important truth: Our lives are a gift from God. We are made in God's image.

When we respect and honor the lives of others, we honor God. When we take care of ourselves and others, we show that we are grateful to God for his gift of life.

The Church teaches that because God has created us, our lives are in his hands. From the very beginning, when we are still inside our mothers, until our death, our lives are sacred. This is why it is so deeply wrong to take another person's life. Everything we do must show respect for life, for all people.

The Church teaches and guides us.

We are members of the Church, the Body of Christ. We work together to follow God's laws of love. The Holy Spirit guides the whole Church. The pope and bishops teach us how to live as God created us to live. This is called the **Magisterium**. It is how the Church teaches and guides us in the truth. It is the teaching office of the Church.

Just as God gives us laws out of love, the Church gives us laws to help us know our basic responsibilities as members of the Church. We call these laws the **Precepts of the Church**. For example, we know that we receive Jesus' life in the Eucharist. This is why the Mass is so important for us. Attending Mass on Sundays and Holy Days of Obligation is a commandment and is a Precept of the Church.

The Precepts of the Church are a good moral starting point for us to grow as God's people. As we grow, we help the Church grow. We spread Jesus' love. This is how we build a better world for all people.

Faith Words

Magisterium the teaching office of the Church

Precepts of the Church laws to help us know our basic responsibilities as members of the Church

Understanding the Precepts of the Church

- We rest and attend Mass on Sundays and on Holy Days of Obligation.

- We confess our sins at least once a year.

- We receive Holy Communion at least during the Easter season.

- We take part in days of fasting and abstinence as we are able.

- We provide for the needs of the Church as we are able.

Activity

The word *Magisterium* comes from the Latin meaning "master," or someone who leads. The pope and bishops make up the Magisterium.

Priests and deacons help the bishops. Do you know the name of your diocese and your bishop? If not, ask your catechist for help. Then complete the sentences.

My diocese is the _____.

My bishop/archbishop is _____.

My priest is _____.

As a group, write a note to your bishop, thanking him for his service to the Church.

Faith Words

Ten Commandments   **prayer**   **worship**
Magisterium   **Precepts of the Church**

 Show What You Know

Complete the sentences.

1. The _____ are laws to help us know our basic responsibilities as members of the Church.

2. When we _____, we are giving God thanks and praise.

3. _____ is listening and talking to God.

4. The _____ are God's laws that were given to Moses, to help people know how to love God and others.

5. The teaching office of the Church is called the

_____.

Partners in Faith

Saint Alphonsus Liguori

When Saint Alphonsus Liguori was named a bishop, he did his best to lead and teach the people in his diocese. He was known for his writing and preaching. He knew that people needed to know the truth of the Gospel.

 Learn more about the life of Saint Alphonsus Liguori.

Copyright © by William H. Sadlier, Inc. All rights reserved.

Original Sin affects all people.

We are all made in God's image. God has given us gifts to help us live in his goodness and love. He has given each of us a soul, a mind, and a conscience. He has given us laws and rules to guide us. We have free will to make our own choices. With all these good gifts from God, we want to do the right thing. But because of Original Sin, we can choose things that are sinful and not good for us.

But God always loves us. Even when we turn from God and sin, he forgives us in the Sacrament of Penance and Reconciliation.

What good choices do I make?

Did You Know?

 Choices have consequences.

Sin harms our relationship with God and one another.

When you are part of a family, you are part of a relationship. Your choices and actions can have an effect on everyone in the family. This is also true with God's family. We have a relationship with God and with one another. The good moral choices we make help us live in a good relationship with God and one another. This is what makes us happy.

Faith Word

sin a thought, word, or action that is against God's law

Sometimes we make choices we know are wrong. These choices are **sins**. A sin is something we do, say, or think that goes against God's laws. A sin is a choice we freely make. That is why mistakes and accidents are not sins.

When we sin, we harm our relationship with God and with one another. We also hurt ourselves. When we sin, we need to ask God to forgive us, so that our relationship with God can be made strong again. We can seek God's forgiveness in the Sacrament of Penance and Reconciliation.

Activity

Think about the choices you make. Write a prayer asking God to help you make good choices.

_____

_____

What are the wrong choices here? Is God offended by these choices? Sometimes a morally wrong choice can be made again and again. These choices harm our relationship with others, even when we do not realize the harm our choice causes. The choices also harm our relationship with God. It is up to us to turn to God, ask for his forgiveness, and make a firm choice to not repeat the wrong action.

We do not ever have to be afraid to confess our sins to God. He always forgives us and gives us strength to do better next time. This is how we can live and grow in God's love.

> *"If we acknowledge our sins, he is faithful and just and will forgive our sins and cleanse us from every wrongdoing."*
>
> *1 John 1:9*

Faith Words

sin   mortal sin   venial sin

 Show What You Know

Read the statements. Circle whether the statement is True or False.
Correct any false statements you find.

1. Mortal sins break our relationship with God.   True / False

_____

_____

2. Sins can be accidents or mistakes.   True / False

_____

_____

3. Venial sins break our relationship with God.   True / False

_____

_____

Partners in Faith

Blessed Anne Mary Taigi

Bad choices can lead to sin, but good choices
lead to holiness. Blessed Anne Mary Taigi
knew that good habits help us become holy.
She became holy by taking care of her family.
She always tried to be cheerful.

 **Learn more about the life of
Blessed Anne Mary Taigi.**

Copyright © by William H. Sadlier, Inc. All rights reserved.

Mini-Task

At the Transfiguration, the Holy Spirit was present in a "bright cloud."

Think about a bright cloud. Write some qualities of a bright cloud.

How is a bright cloud like the Holy Spirit?

Turn and talk to a partner.

Imagine you are designing a product for kids that would remind them of the Holy Spirit as a bright cloud. It may be something they wear on their clothing or something they carry with them. It must remind them that the Holy Spirit is always with them.

What would you design?

What would your design look like?

 Want to do more? Go to your Portfolio to continue this activity.

At  Home

Together with your family, share a time when you were strengthened by God's grace.

Copyright © by William H. Sadlier, Inc. All rights reserved.

How do we become what we believe?

Jesus Enters Jerusalem

Unit Prayer

Leader: Venerable Pierre Toussaint cherished his Catholic faith by attending daily Mass. He knew that prayer is important in our daily lives, especially when we are all together in class, in church, and at home.

Let us listen to stories about prayer. Listen to the stories of missionary disciples today.

Leader: Let us pray:
We pray for peace in the world for all people.
O Lord, grant us your peace.

All: O Lord, grant us your peace.

Leader: We pray for peace in our homes and in our hearts.

All: O Lord, grant us your peace.

Leader: We pray for the Church and Church leaders.

All: O Lord, grant us your peace.

Leader: Let us pray for peace among families.

All: O Lord, grant us your peace.

Leader: Let us pray the Lord's Prayer.

All: Our Father, . . .

End the Unit Prayer by singing the song for this unit.

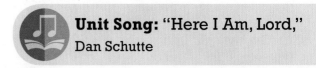

Unit Song: "Here I Am, Lord," Dan Schutte

Missionary Discipleship

How does prayer help us and others to know Jesus? Share a story about a time when you prayed with someone else. How did you feel?

What is prayer?

God desires to be with us! He is always calling us to prayer. We pray by listening to God and speaking to him from our hearts. The Church helps us pray so that we can grow closer to God.

 Go to the digital portal for a prayer of praise.

"The Lord is near to all who call upon him, to all who call upon him in truth."

Psalm 145:18

Mini-Task

A recipe is a set of ingredients and instructions that come together, usually in a food dish. But you can also think of a recipe for other outcomes beyond cooking. Imagine that you have been asked to write a "recipe for prayer" that will offer ways to be closer to God.

RECIPE

INGREDIENTS

1. _____
2. _____
3. _____
4. _____
5. _____
6. _____

STEPS

1. _____
_____
2. _____
_____
3. _____
_____

What are the "ingredients" needed for prayer?

These might include a quiet place away from everyday noise. What are other steps a person might take to pray and be closer to God?

Complete the recipe card.

Trade your card with a partner, and see if he or she can follow the recipe to pray and be closer to God.

 Want to do more? Go to your Portfolio to continue this activity.

 **At Home**

Together as a family, find the Book of Psalms in the Bible. Pray one of the Psalms mentioned in this lesson: 2, 62, 103, 121, or 130. Take turns praying different lines of the psalm. Which lines speak to you as a family?

Copyright © by William H. Sadlier, Inc. All rights reserved.

Why do we pray?

We are made in God's image and likeness. By the gift of faith, we believe in God and pray to him. We pray to grow closer to God. We pray to be more like Jesus. The Holy Spirit guides the Church's prayer through Sacred Tradition. When we pray at all times and in all places, our love and trust in God grow, and we become more like Christ.

Go to the digital portal for a prayer of petition.

"The fervent prayer of a righteous person is very powerful."

James 5:16

What do I ask God for in prayer?

Mini-Task

At Mass, we pray prayers of petition together. After each petition, we ask God to hear our prayer with the words "Lord, hear our prayer." Imagine you have been asked to write the petitions for next Sunday's Mass.

In the prayer book page, write petitions for each of the topics.

Share your prayer with the group or at home. Invite your group members to respond by saying "Lord, hear our prayer" after each petition.

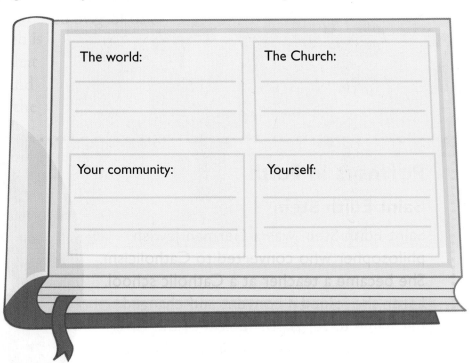

The world: _____

The Church: _____

Your community: _____

Yourself: _____

 Want to do more? Go to your Portfolio to continue this activity.

 At Home

In prayers of petition, we ask God for help. With your family, write about or draw pictures of something you need help with. Take quiet time together to pray a prayer of petition for help with these things.

Copyright © by William H. Sadlier, Inc. All rights reserved.

How do we pray?

We pray every day. We can say prayers of blessing and thanksgiving. We can ask God for good things for ourselves and for others. We can pray out loud and in silence, with others and by ourselves. We can use prayers we have memorized, and we can pray in our own words. No matter how we pray, the Holy Spirit is at work in our prayer, helping us grow in our faith.

 Go to the digital portal for a prayer of intercession.

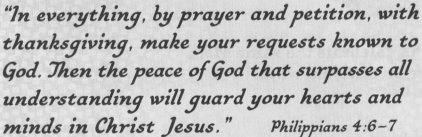 *"In everything, by prayer and petition, with thanksgiving, make your requests known to God. Then the peace of God that surpasses all understanding will guard your hearts and minds in Christ Jesus."* Philippians 4:6–7

Mini-Task

Write a paragraph that supports the statement below. Go back into your lesson to review what you learned in this lesson. Make notes or highlight information and key ideas that you will use.

When we pray the Our Father, we live out the way to follow Jesus.

_____

_____

_____

_____

_____

_____

_____

_____

Read your paragraph to a partner and listen to his or her paragraph. Have a discussion about what you both wrote. Your paragraph has been inspired by your praying the Lord's Prayer. How will your paragraph inspire others to follow Jesus?

 Want to do more? Go to your Portfolio to continue this activity.

 **At Home**

Have each member of your family copy some favorite words or phrases from the Our Father onto small pieces of paper or cards. Decorate the cards as a family. Pray the Our Father together while you hold your cards.

Copyright © by William H. Sadlier, Inc. All rights reserved.

Why and how do we celebrate the Church year?

Unit 5

Seasons and Feasts of the Church Year

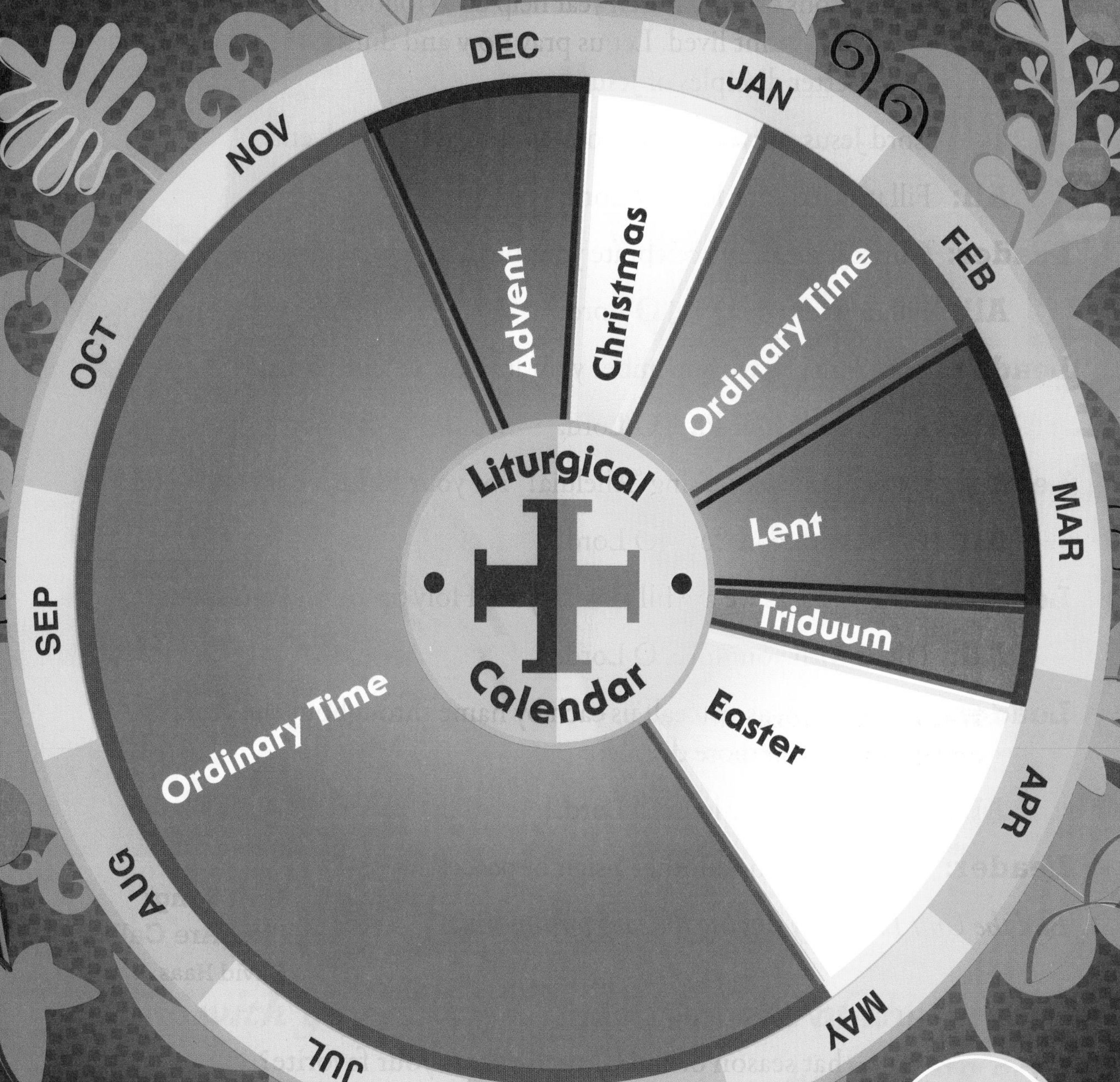

Liturgical Calendar
DEC
JAN
FEB
MAR
APR
MAY
JUN
JUL
AUG
SEP
OCT
NOV
Advent
Christmas
Ordinary Time
Lent
Triduum
Easter
Ordinary Time

Church Year Prayer Ritual

 "Forever Will I Sing," Ed Bolduc

Leader: The liturgical year is a gift to us from the Church, and it follows the life, Death, and Resurrection of Jesus. It flows like a river through the seasons of the year: fall, winter, spring, and summer. Each of the seasons of the liturgical year, like each season of the earth, shows us the beauty of God in all things.

We celebrate the Eucharist in these seasons, giving thanks and praise to God for his love for us through Jesus, his Son, and for sending us his Holy Spirit.

As we celebrate the seasons of the liturgical year, make the Sign of the Cross. In the name of the Father, . . .

Let us thank God for the season of Advent. We prepare for the coming of Jesus at Christmas in our homes and in the world. We make a place for his coming in our hearts, that we might know Jesus' love for us in a new way.

All: We celebrate Christ in us.

Leader: Let us thank God for the season of Christmas. We celebrate this beautiful time by sharing gifts with our families and friends. We celebrate with special meals and music.

All: We celebrate Christ in us.

Leader: We thank God for the season of Lent. Like Advent, we prepare for something else to come during Lent. We prepare for the Death and Resurrection of Jesus at Easter. We pray and do other special actions that help us focus on Jesus' love for us.

All: We celebrate Christ in us.

Leader: We thank you, God, for the season of Easter and for Pentecost. We know your presence in our lives as Father, Son, and Holy Spirit. The Sacraments of Baptism, Confirmation, the Eucharist, and Penance and Reconciliation help us bring the light of Christ to the world. Let us be the light of Christ that is in us.

All: We celebrate Christ in us.

Leader: As the candle is passed to you, say "Let us be the light of Christ who is in us!"

(*Pass a battery-lighted or unlit candle to all in the room.*)

Leader: We will now pray together in the words Jesus taught us:

All: Our Father, who art in heaven,
hallowed be thy name;
thy kingdom come;
thy will be done on earth as it is in heaven.
Give us this day our daily bread;
and forgive us our trespasses
as we forgive those who trespass against us;
and lead us not into temptation,
but deliver us from evil. Amen.

How do I celebrate Jesus all year?

Mini-Task

The seasons of the Church year help us celebrate Jesus' life and work. All year, we can share what we know about Jesus' life and work with others.

As you learn about the seasons of the Church year, you are going to write clues that could be used in a guessing game. These clues will also help you as you celebrate the Church year. For each season you learn about, you will write three new clues.

As your collection of clues grows, you can play your guessing game with family and friends.

In the spaces below, write three clues about the Church year. You can use words or pictures as your clues.

Clue 1:	Clue 2:	Clue 3:	Answer: The Church Year

Test your clues on a friend. Can your friend guess the answer with the clues you made?

 Want to do more? Go to your Portfolio to continue this activity.

Invite each member of your family to talk about a way he or she saw God's love in the world today. Pray a prayer of thanks to God for sharing his love in these ways.

Copyright © by William H. Sadlier, Inc. All rights reserved.

Why does Jesus come to save us?

Advent

"Amen! Come, Lord Jesus!"

Revelation 22:20

Triduum Prayer Ritual

 "I Have Loved You," Michael Joncas

Leader: In the name of the Father, and of the Son, and of the Holy Spirit. Amen.

During Holy Week, we celebrate the three days of the Triduum. On Holy Thursday, we celebrate the Mass of the Lord's Supper. On Good Friday, we remember the events of Jesus' suffering and Death on the Cross. The liturgy of the Easter Vigil begins in darkness, before we light the Easter candle and celebrate Jesus' Resurrection!

All: Let all creation praise the name of the Risen Lord.

Leader: Come forward now to the bowl of holy water and bless yourself.

Let us now ask God to hear our prayers:

We pray for the Church, that the events of the Triduum inspire us to be the light of Christ in the world.

All: Lord, hear our prayer.

Leader: We pray that the suffering and Death of Jesus remind us to trust in you and thank you for the gift of your Son.

All: Lord, hear our prayer.

Leader: We pray that Jesus' Resurrection reminds us to have hope in new life and to live as Christ taught: "Love one another as I have loved you."

All: Lord, hear our prayer.

Leader: Let us say a prayer from the Easter Vigil as we light this candle.

(*Pass a candle around your circle.*)

May the light of Christ rising in glory

All: May the light of Christ rising in glory

Leader: clear the darkness from our hearts and minds.

All: clear the darkness from our hearts and minds.

Leader: The light of Christ.

All: Thanks be to God.

Triduum

Why did Jesus die on the Cross and rise again?

Mini-Task

During the days of the Triduum, we remember the events of the Last Supper and Jesus' suffering, Death, and Resurrection.

Remember what you learned and experienced in this lesson about the days of the Triduum. In the space below, write three clues about the three days. You can use words or pictures as your clues.

Clue 1:	Clue 2:	Clue 3:	Answer: Triduum

Test your clues on a friend. Can your friend guess the answer with the clues you made? To make a guessing game, combine these clues with any other Church year clues you have already written.

 Want to do more? Go to your Portfolio to continue this activity.

 At Home

If you have a cross in your home, pray before it tonight as a family. If you do not have a cross at home, cut a cross shape out of a sheet of paper and post it somewhere in your home where you can pray.

Copyright © by William H. Sadlier, Inc. All rights reserved.

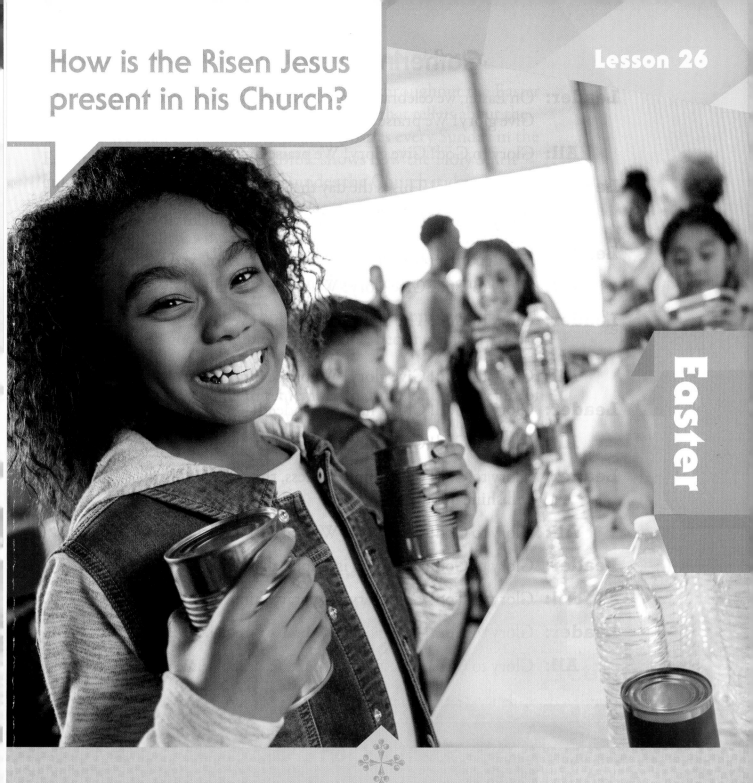

How is the Risen Jesus present in his Church?

Easter

"With great power the apostles bore witness to the resurrection of the Lord Jesus."

Acts of the Apostles 4:33

Gathering Prayer

Leader: On the great feast of Pentecost, we ask the Holy Spirit to come to us, that we might be filled with God's love and share it with the world!

Come, Holy Spirit, and fill our hearts with your strength.

All: Come, Holy Spirit, and fill our hearts with your strength.

Leader: Come, Holy Spirit, wash over us with your peace.

All: Come, Holy Spirit, wash over us with your peace.

Leader: Come, Holy Spirit, and renew the face of the earth.

All: Come, Holy Spirit, and renew the face of the earth.

Leader: Come, Holy Spirit, enlighten our minds.

All: Come, Holy Spirit, enlighten our minds.

Leader: Come, Holy Spirit, give us the faith to share Christ in us with one another.

All: Come, Holy Spirit, give us the faith to share Christ in us with one another.

Activity

To enlighten means "to make something clearer or more understandable." You can enlighten others about your Catholic faith! Choose one of these things you have learned about Jesus. Ask the Holy Spirit to help you explain your answer to a friend.

- Jesus is divine and human.

- Jesus is Son of God and the son of Mary.

- The Blessed Trinity is One God in Three Persons.

Pentecost was the beginning of the Church's public ministry.

Pentecost Sunday is very important to the life of the Church. In the Pentecost liturgy, we learn how the followers of Jesus received the Holy Spirit at the first Pentecost. The Holy Spirit is still active in the Church.

The Holy Spirit brings the followers of Jesus together. Through the Holy Spirit, the Third Person of the Blessed Trinity, we are united as one body in one community of faith. The Church is one and receives her life from the Holy Spirit.

The Holy Spirit sends the Church out to proclaim the Good News, without fear. We are sent to share the love of Jesus with the whole world.

On the day of Pentecost, Saint Peter preached to the crowds, and many people believed in Jesus. The Church today continues to invite everyone to believe that Jesus is the Savior of the world.

The Holy Spirit gives us the gift of understanding to help us recognize all that Christ did for our salvation.

Did You Know?

 We are called to preach.

Activity

Name one place you visit often, such as school, a soccer or skating park, or a community center. How can you tell people you meet there about Jesus?

_____

_____

_____

Readers Theater

The Disciples Spread the Good News of Jesus

Acts of the Apostles 2:4–13, 37–41

Roles: Narrator 1; Narrator 2; Narrator 3; Narrator 4; Persons 1, 2, 3, and 4; Peter

After the Holy Spirit came upon the disciples, they went out and spread the Good News.

Narrator 1: The Holy Spirit came down upon the disciples as tongues of fire.

Narrator 2: The disciples were filled with the Spirit and began to speak in different languages.

Narrator 3: The Spirit had enabled the disciples to proclaim the Good News.

Narrator 4: The Holy Spirit had given them courage and the strength to go out and preach to the people.

Narrator 1: Now at that time, there were devout Jews from every nation under heaven staying in Jerusalem. They were gathered outside in a large crowd.

Narrator 2: The people heard the disciples speaking, but they were confused because each one heard the disciples speaking in his own language. In amazement they asked:

Person 1: "Are not all these people who are speaking Galileans? Then how does each of us hear them in his own native language?"

Person 2: "We are Parthians, Medes, and Elamites, inhabitants of Mesopotamia, Judea and Cappadocia, Pontus and Asia, Phrygia and Pamphylia,"

Person 3: "Egypt and the districts of Libya near Cyrene, as well as travelers from Rome, both Jews and converts to Judaism, Cretans and Arabs,"

Person 4: "Yet we hear them speaking in our own tongues of the mighty acts of God" (Acts of the Apostles 2:7–11).

Narrator 1: The people were all astounded and bewildered, and said to one another:

Persons 1/2: "What does this mean?" (Acts of the Apostles 2:12).

Narrator 2: But others said, scoffing:

Persons 3/4: "They have had too much new wine" (Acts of the Apostles 2:13).

Narrator 3: Then Peter arose to speak in a loud, strong voice. He quoted many words from Scripture. He told the people:

Peter: "Repent and be baptized, every one of you, in the name of Jesus Christ for the forgiveness of your sins; and you will receive the gift of the holy Spirit" (Acts of the Apostles 2:38).

Narrator 4: Those who accepted his message were baptized, and about three thousand persons became followers of Jesus that day.

Who is the Holy Spirit?

Mini-Task

On Pentecost, we remember the Holy Spirit coming to the Apostles, giving them the power to share what they knew about Jesus.

Remember what you learned and experienced in this lesson about Pentecost. In the space below, write three clues about Pentecost. You can use words or pictures as your clues.

Clue 1:	Clue 2:	Clue 3:	Answer: Pentecost

Test your clues on a friend. Can your friend guess the answer with the clues you made? To make a guessing game, combine these clues with any other Church year clues you have already written.

 Want to do more? Go to your Portfolio to continue this activity.

At Home

As a family, talk about ways you can invite others to become part of Jesus' Church through your words and actions. Choose something you can do now.

Copyright © by William H. Sadlier, Inc. All rights reserved.

How do we grow as Jesus' followers?

Ordinary Time

"The one who began a good work in you will continue to complete it." *Philippians 1:6*

Gathering Prayer

Leader: Ordinary Time is the longest season of the Church year. During this season, the Church spends time reading and listening to the stories of Jesus' life and work. Jesus is our role model, our best example of how to love and trust in God. Jesus gave us the Church so we could learn from him to love God.

We praise God for the gift of the Church.

All: O God, we praise you for the Church.

Leader: For the stories we read in the Word of God at church:

All: O God, we praise you for the Church.

Leader: For the pope, bishops, and other leaders:

All: O God, we praise you for the Church.

Leader: For our priests and deacons, who guide our parish:

All: O God, we praise you for the Church.

Leader: For the people of our parish, who are our good examples:

All: O God, we praise you for the Church.

Leader: Praise to you, O God, for the gift of our Church in Ordinary Time and all year round.

All: O God, we praise you for the Church.

Activity

Sometimes we feel sad after joyful seasons like Christmas and Easter are over. How can we stay joyful? Talk with your group about some things you can do to show how happy Jesus makes us all year long. Write one idea here:

_____

_____

_____

We learn about Jesus and his teachings during Ordinary Time.

The longest season of the Church year is Ordinary Time. It is thirty-three or thirty-four weeks long. During Ordinary Time, we accompany Jesus on his earthly mission, witness his ministry, and learn his teachings.

During his earthly ministry, Jesus called the first disciples, Andrew and Simon Peter (John 1:35–42). He taught about the Father's love and invited people to hear and believe and to follow him. Jesus calls us to be his faith-filled followers, too.

Throughout Ordinary Time, we learn about Jesus. We listen to his teachings in the Gospels. We hear accounts of Jesus' healing miracles and his works of mercy. Through the Scripture readings we hear at Mass and the Church's teaching, we learn what is asked of us as disciples.

Ordinary Time is a season to learn more about our faith, day by day, and to imitate Jesus through prayer and loving actions.

Did You Know?

 We become what we practice.

Activity

Draw something that grows from a small size to a large size over time, like a plant. On the different stages of growth, write some good and loving actions that help to grow the Kingdom of God.

Ordinary Time Prayer Ritual

 "Prayer of St. Francis," Sebastian Temple

Leader: In the name of the Father, and of the Son, and of the Holy Spirit. Amen.

During the season of Ordinary Time, we are taught by Jesus just as he taught his disciples. We, too, can be disciples of Jesus by listening to his teachings and living as Christ has taught. By listening and then by doing what Jesus teaches, we are able to share Christ, who is alive in us, with the world!

The Scriptures that are proclaimed during Mass during Ordinary Time are hardly ordinary, as they often tell of Jesus performing miracles, such as healing the sick, raising the dead, and restoring vision to the blind. You might say this could be "extraordinary" time!

In order for us to really "hear," we must really "listen." Listen now to a passage from the Gospel of Mark.

Reader: The people brought a deaf man to Jesus who also had a problem speaking, who begged Jesus to heal him. "[Jesus] put his finger into the man's ears and . . . touched his tongue; then he looked up to heaven . . . and said to him, '*Ephphatha!*' (that is, 'Be opened!') And [immediately] the man's ears were opened, . . . and he spoke plainly." Jesus' followers said: "He has done all things well. He makes the deaf hear and [the] mute speak" (Mark 7:33–35, 37).

Leader: Let us take a few minutes to think about the times in our lives when we have not listened to our parents and the times we have spoken words that we regretted.

(Share reflections as instrumental music plays.)

Leader: Let us pray:

For the times we have seen others who need our help but have turned away.

Trace a Sign of the Cross on your eyes as we pray: "Open our eyes, Lord."

All: Open our eyes, Lord.

Leader: For the times that we have been asked to help but have turned away.

Trace a Sign of the Cross on your ears as we pray: "Open our ears, Lord."

All: Open our ears, Lord.

Leader: For the times that we have hurt others by our actions.

Trace a Sign of the Cross on your heart as we pray: "Open our hearts, Lord."

All: Open our hearts, Lord.

Leader: Let us sing the song "Prayer of St. Francis."

(All sing.)

Leader: Let us offer one another a sign of peace.

How do we grow as Jesus' followers?

Mini-Task

During Ordinary Time, we listen to Jesus' teachings and imitate Jesus through prayer and loving actions.

Remember what you learned and experienced in this lesson about the season of Ordinary Time. In the space below, write three clues about Ordinary Time. You can use words or pictures as your clues.

Clue 1:	Clue 2:	Clue 3:	Answer: Ordinary Time

Test your clues on a friend. Can your friend guess the answer with the clues you made?

 Want to do more? Go to your Portfolio to continue this activity.

 **At Home**

Talk with family members about how you have imitated Jesus this week through your prayers and loving actions. Choose something new you can do next week.

Copyright © by William H. Sadlier, Inc. All rights reserved.

Welcome

to your *Christ In Us* Sourcebook

My Prayers...236

How to Pray the Rosary.....................................239

The Sanctuary...240

Ten Commandments, Beatitudes, Sacraments, Great Commandment........242

My *Christ In Us* Mass Book.................................243

Stations of the Cross......................................247

Celebrating Penance and Reconciliation.....................248

Examination of Conscience..................................249

How to Receive Holy Communion..............................250

Family Companion..251

What—or Who—Is the Church?.................................252

Praying with Mary, Messengers of God.......................253

The Seven Themes of Catholic Social Teaching...............254

Interfaith Dialogue.......................................255

The Communion of Saints—The Canonization Process..........256

Glossary..257

Q & A...260

Index...266

Sign of the Cross

In the name of the Father,
and of the Son,
and of the Holy Spirit.
Amen.

Our Father

Our Father, who art in heaven,
hallowed be thy name;
thy kingdom come;
thy will be done on earth as
    it is in heaven.
Give us this day our daily bread;
and forgive us our trespasses
as we forgive those who
    trespass against us;
and lead us not into
temptation,
but deliver us from evil.
Amen.

Hail Mary

Hail Mary, full of grace,
the Lord is with you!
Blessed are you among women,
and blessed is the fruit of
    your womb, Jesus.
Holy Mary, Mother of God,
pray for us sinners,
now and at the hour of our death.
Amen.

Glory Be to the Father

Glory be to the Father
and to the Son
and to the Holy Spirit,
as it was in the beginning,
is now, and ever shall be,
world without end.
Amen.

Jesus Prayer

Lord Jesus Christ,
Son of God, have mercy on me,
a sinner.

Act of Faith

Oh God, we believe in all that Jesus has
taught us about you. We place all our
trust in you because of your great love
for us.

Act of Hope

Oh God, we never give up on your love.
We have hope and will work for your
Kingdom to come and for a life that
lasts forever with you in heaven.

Act of Love

Oh God, we love you above all things.
Help us to love ourselves and one
another as Jesus taught us to do.

Act of Contrition

My God,
I am sorry for my sins with
    all my heart.
In choosing to do wrong
and failing to do good,
I have sinned against you
whom I should love above
    all things.
I firmly intend, with your help,
to do penance,
to sin no more,
and to avoid whatever
    leads me to sin.
Our Savior Jesus Christ
suffered and died for us.
In his name, my God,
    have mercy.
Amen.

Morning Offering

O Jesus, I offer you all my prayers, works,
and sufferings of this day for all the
    intentions of your most Sacred Heart.
Amen.

Evening Prayer

Dear God, before I sleep
I want to thank you for this day,
so full of your kindness
and your joy.
I close my eyes to rest
safe in your loving care.

Prayer of Saint Benedict

Gracious and holy Father,
grant us the intellect to understand you,
reason to discern you, diligence to
    seek you,
wisdom to find you, a spirit to
    know you,
a heart to meditate upon you.
May our ears hear you, may our eyes
    behold you,
and may our tongues proclaim you.
Give us grace that our way of life may
    be pleasing to you,
    that we may have the patience to
    wait for you
and the perseverance to look for you.
Grant us a perfect end—your holy
    presence,
a blessed resurrection, and life
    everlasting.
We ask this through Jesus Christ
    our Lord.

Apostles' Creed

I believe in God, the Father almighty,
    Creator of heaven and earth,
and in Jesus Christ, his only Son,
    our Lord,
who was conceived by the Holy Spirit,
born of the Virgin Mary,
suffered under Pontius Pilate,
was crucified, died and was buried;
he descended into hell;
on the third day he rose again
from the dead;
he ascended into heaven,
and is seated at the right hand
    of God the Father almighty;
from there he will come to judge
    the living and the dead.
I believe in the Holy Spirit,
    the holy catholic Church,
    the communion of saints,
    the forgiveness of sins,
    the resurrection of the body,
    and life everlasting. Amen.

Hail, Holy Queen

Hail, holy Queen, mother of mercy,
hail, our life, our sweetness, and
    our hope.
To you we cry, the children of Eve;
to you we send up our sighs,
mourning and weeping in this land
    of exile.
Turn, then, most gracious advocate,
your eyes of mercy toward us;
lead us home at last and show us
the blessed fruit of your womb,
Jesus: O clement, O loving, O sweet
    Virgin Mary.

Grace Before Meals

Bless us, O Lord,
    and these your gifts
which we are about to receive
from your goodness.
Through Christ our Lord.
Amen.

Grace After Meals

We give you thanks, almighty God,
for these and all your gifts,
which we have received through
Christ our Lord.
Amen.

Prayer Before the Blessed Sacrament

Jesus,
You are God-with-us,
especially in this sacrament
of the Eucharist.
You love me as I am
and help me grow.

Come and be with me
in all my joys and sorrows.
Help me share your peace and love
with everyone I meet.
I ask in your name.
Amen.

How to Pray the Rosary

A rosary is made up of groups of beads arranged in a circle. It begins with a cross followed by one large bead and three small ones. The next large bead (just before the medal) begins the first "decade." Each decade consists of one large bead followed by ten smaller beads.

Begin to pray the Rosary with the Sign of the Cross. Recite the Apostles' Creed. Then pray one Our Father, three Hail Marys, and one Glory Be to the Father.

To pray each decade, say an Our Father on the large bead and a Hail Mary on each of the ten smaller beads. Close each decade by praying the Glory Be to the Father. Pray the Hail, Holy Queen as the last prayer of the Rosary.

The mysteries of the Rosary are special events in the lives of Jesus and Mary. As you pray each decade, think of the appropriate Joyful Mystery, Sorrowful Mystery, Glorious Mystery, or Mystery of Light.

The Five Joyful Mysteries
1. The Annunciation
2. The Visitation
3. The Birth of Jesus
4. The Presentation of Jesus in the Temple
5. The Finding of Jesus in the Temple

The Five Sorrowful Mysteries
1. The Agony in the Garden
2. The Scourging at the Pillar
3. The Crowning with Thorns
4. The Carrying of the Cross
5. The Crucifixion and Death of Jesus

The Five Glorious Mysteries
1. The Resurrection
2. The Ascension
3. The Descent of the Holy Spirit upon the Apostles
4. The Assumption of Mary into Heaven
5. The Coronation of Mary as Queen of Heaven

The Five Mysteries of Light
1. Jesus' Baptism in the Jordan
2. The Miracle at the Wedding at Cana
3. Jesus Announces the Kingdom of God
4. The Transfiguration
5. The Institution of the Eucharist

1 **sanctuary** the part of the church that includes the altar and the ambo. The word *sanctuary* means "holy place."

2 **altar** the special table that is the center of the celebration of the Liturgy of the Eucharist, also called the Table of the Lord.

3 **crucifix** a cross with a figure of Christ crucified, displayed in the sanctuary.

4 **tabernacle** the special place in the church in which the Most Blessed Sacrament is placed in reserve.

5 **sanctuary lamp** light or candle that is always lit near the tabernacle. It helps us to remember that Jesus is really present in the Most Blessed Sacrament.

6 **ambo** a sacred reading stand called the Table of the Word of God. The ambo is used only for proclamation of the Scripture in the liturgy.

7 **chalice** the special cup into which the priest pours grape wine that becomes the Blood of Christ during the Liturgy of the Eucharist.

8 **paten** the special plate on which the priest places the wheat bread that becomes the Body of Christ during the Liturgy of the Eucharist.

9 **cruets** small glass jars that contain the water and the grape wine used at Mass.

10 **presider's chair** chair on which the priest who is celebrating Mass sits.

11 processional cross cross with a figure of Christ crucified that is carried in the entrance procession and may also be carried during the Offertory procession and during the recessional.

12 paschal candle a large candle that is blessed and lit every Easter. The lighted paschal candle represents the Risen Christ among us. The flame of the paschal candle is used to light baptismal candles.

13 baptismal font or pool contains the water that is blessed and used during the Sacrament of Baptism.

14 Stations of the Cross fourteen pictures that help us to follow the footsteps of Jesus during his Passion and Death on the Cross.

15 Reconciliation Room or confessional a separate space for celebrating the Sacrament of Penance and Reconciliation. This is where you meet the priest for individual confession and absolution. You may sit and talk to him face-to-face or kneel behind a screen.

16 stained glass colorful windows that may show saints or scenes from Scripture.

17 pews where the assembly is seated during the celebration of Mass.

18 statue of Mary image of the Mother of God, our greatest saint. Statues of other saints may also be found in the church.

241

The Ten Commandments

1. I am the LORD your God: you shall not have strange gods before me.
2. You shall not take the name of the LORD your God in vain.
3. Remember to keep holy the LORD's Day.
4. Honor your father and your mother.
5. You shall not kill.
6. You shall not commit adultery.
7. You shall not steal.
8. You shall not bear false witness against your neighbor.
9. You shall not covet your neighbor's wife.
10. You shall not covet your neighbor's goods.

The Seven Sacraments

The Sacraments of Christian Initiation

Baptism
Confirmation
Eucharist

The Sacraments of Healing

Penance and Reconciliation
Anointing of the Sick

The Sacraments at the Service of Communion

Holy Orders
Matrimony

The Great Commandment

"You shall love the Lord, your God, with all your heart, with all your soul, and with all your mind. This is the greatest and the first commandment. The second is like it: You shall love your neighbor as yourself."

Matthew 22:37–39

The Beatitudes

"Blessed are the poor in spirit, for theirs is the kingdom of heaven."
"Blessed are they who mourn, for they will be comforted."
"Blessed are the meek, for they will inherit the land."
"Blessed are they who hunger and thirst for righteousness, for they will be satisfied."
"Blessed are the merciful, for they will be shown mercy."
"Blessed are the clean of heart, for they will see God."
"Blessed are the peacemakers, for they will be called children of God."
"Blessed are they who are persecuted for the sake of righteousness, for theirs is the kingdom of heaven."

Matthew 5:3–10

Fold on this line.

Cut on this line.

My ✤ Mass Book

Concluding Rites

The priest blesses us. The priest or deacon may say "Go in peace."
We say: **"Thanks be to God."**

We stand and sing a gathering song. We pray the Sign of the Cross. The priest says: "The Lord be with you." We answer: **"And with your spirit."** We ask God and one another for forgiveness.

Introductory Rite

We gather with our parish to worship God. We remember and celebrate what Jesus said and did at the Last Supper.

2

Cut on this line.

Fold on this line.

We go out to live as Jesus' followers.

15

We praise God as we sing or say: **"Glory to God in the highest, and on earth peace to people of good will."**

4

Then the priest invites us to share in the Eucharist. As people receive the Body and Blood of Christ, they answer: **"Amen."** While this is happening, we sing a song of thanks.

13

We get ready to receive Jesus. Together we pray or sing the Our Father. Then we share a sign of peace. We say: "**Peace be with you.**"

12

The Liturgy of the Word

We listen to two readings from the Bible, from the Old Testament and the New Testament. After each one, the reader says: "The word of the Lord." We answer: "**Thanks be to God.**"

5

Fold on this line.

Cut on this line.

Then the priest takes the cup of wine. He says: "Take this, all of you, and drink from it, for this is the chalice of my Blood...."

10

We stand to say aloud what we believe as Catholics. Then we pray for the Church and all God's people. After each prayer we say: "**Lord, hear our prayer.**"

7

We stand and sing Alleluia. The priest or deacon reads the Gospel. Then he says: **"The Gospel of the Lord."**
We answer: **"Praise to you, Lord Jesus Christ."**

Cut on this line.

The Liturgy of the Eucharist

The priest prepares the altar. People bring gifts of bread and wine to the priest. The priest prepares these gifts. We pray: **"Blessed be God for ever."**

We sing or pray: **"Amen."** We believe Jesus Christ is really present in the Eucharist.

Then we remember what Jesus said and did at the Last Supper. The priest takes the bread. He says: "TAKE THIS, ALL OF YOU, AND EAT OF IT, FOR THIS IS MY BODY, WHICH WILL BE GIVEN UP FOR YOU."

Fold on this line.

Stations of the Cross

In the Stations of the Cross, we follow in the footsteps of Jesus during his Passion and Death on the Cross.

1. Jesus is condemned to die.
2. Jesus takes up his cross.
3. Jesus falls the first time.
4. Jesus meets his mother.
5. Simon helps Jesus carry his cross.
6. Veronica wipes the face of Jesus.
7. Jesus falls the second time.
8. Jesus meets the women of Jerusalem.
9. Jesus falls the third time.

10. Jesus is stripped of his garments.
11. Jesus is nailed to the cross.
12. Jesus dies on the cross.
13. Jesus is taken down from the cross.
14. Jesus is laid in the tomb.

Celebrating Penance and Reconciliation

How do we show God we are sorry? When we receive the Sacrament of Penance and Reconciliation, we show that we are sorry for our sins by confessing them to the priest and doing the penance we receive. Another name for showing we are sorry is repentance. Review the steps to receive the Sacrament of Penance below. Make a commitment with your parents to receive the Sacrament of Penance at least once a year.

Steps to Receive the Sacrament of Penance

- The priest welcomes me, and we both make the Sign of the Cross.

- Sometimes the priest reads a story from the Bible about God's forgiveness.

- I confess my sins to the priest.

- The priest may talk to me about what I can do to make the right choices. He will give me a penance to do. A penance is a prayer or action that shows I am sorry for my sins. I will carry out my penance after the celebration of the sacrament.

- I pray the Act of Contrition, expressing my sorrow for my sins and my intention to avoid sin in the future.

- I receive absolution, or forgiveness, from my sins.

- I join the priest in giving thanks for God's forgiveness.

Examination of Conscience

Before you go to confession, it is helpful to quietly sit and examine your conscience. Use these questions to help you reflect on your relationship with God and others.

Do I make anyone or anything more important to me than God?

Have I read from the Bible and prayed?

Do I respect God's name and the name of Jesus?

Do I participate in Mass and keep Sunday holy by what I say and do?

Do I show obedience to God by my obedience to parents, guardians, and teachers?

Have I hurt others by my words and actions? Have I helped those in need?

Do I respect myself? Do I take good care of my body and show respect to others? Do I respect the dignity of everyone I meet?

Have I been selfish or taken the belongings of others without their permission? Have I shared my belongings?

Have I been honest? Have I lied or cheated?

Do I speak, act, and dress in ways that show respect for myself and others?

Have I been happy for others when they have the things they want or need?

How to Receive Holy Communion

When I receive the consecrated bread, or Host, this is what I do:

I process to the altar with hands joined in prayer.

When my turn comes, the priest, deacon, or extraordinary minister of Holy Communion raises the Host, and I bow my head.

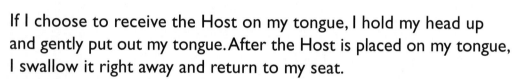

When I hear the words "The Body of Christ," I respond "Amen." I can choose to receive the Host in my hand or on my tongue.

If I choose to receive the Host in my hand, I place my left hand on top of my right hand (or the opposite if I am left-handed). After the Host is placed in my hand, I eat it right away, fold my hands in prayer, and return to my seat.

If I choose to receive the Host on my tongue, I hold my head up and gently put out my tongue. After the Host is placed on my tongue, I swallow it right away and return to my seat.

If I am going to receive from the chalice, I first swallow the Host. I walk to the priest, deacon, or extraordinary minister of Holy Communion holding the chalice.

The chalice is raised before me, and I bow my head.

When I hear the words "The Blood of Christ," I respond "Amen." Then I take a sip from the chalice. After I receive from the chalice, I fold my hands in prayer and return to my seat. I spend time in quiet prayer.

As a sign of respect and reverence for Jesus in the Eucharist, we must have not eaten any food or drink for one hour before receiving Holy Communion. This is called the eucharistic fast. Water and medicine may be taken during the eucharistic fast.

Receive Holy Communion often and the Sacrament of Penance and Reconciliation regularly. When we receive Holy Communion, we must always be in a state of grace. Anyone who has committed a mortal sin must receive absolution in the Sacrament of Penance and Reconciliation before receiving Holy Communion.

Your *Christ In Us*

Family Companion

Welcome. We are so glad that you are a ***Christ In Us*** family! In this section, you will find a treasury of resources as your family accompanies your child on our journey to a greater love in Jesus Christ. This material is written specifically for you as adult family members. But be certain that you review your child's resources that precede this section. Also, don't forget to look over the *Glossary* that follows. It will give you a good oversight of what your child has been experiencing this year. Finally, the *Q&A* offers a wonderful opportunity for your entire family to review the major faith statements of the grade.

What—or Who—Is the Church?

Church can mean a building where we worship, but it also means all baptized believers. Members of the Catholic Church are called the People of God. When Catholics gather at parishes around the world for Mass each Sunday, we are all worshiping together as one Church. The Church is universal, or *catholic*, which means it is open to all people everywhere. Jesus Christ is the head of the Church. We are holy because he is holy. Our faith was handed down to us from the Apostles, whom Jesus chose as the first leaders of the Church.

As you pray the Nicene Creed at Mass on Sunday, reflect with your child on what it means when we say we are one, holy, catholic, and apostolic.

Nicene Creed

I believe in one God,
   the Father almighty,
   maker of heaven and earth,
   of all things visible and invisible.
I believe in one Lord Jesus Christ,
   the Only Begotten Son of God,
   born of the Father before all ages.
   God from God, Light from Light,
   true God from true God,
   begotten, not made, consubstantial
      with the Father;
   through him all things were made.
For us men and for our salvation
   he came down from heaven,
and by the Holy Spirit
   was incarnate of the Virgin Mary,
      and became man.
For our sake he was crucified
      under Pontius Pilate,
he suffered death and was buried,
and rose again on the third day
   in accordance with the Scriptures.
He ascended into heaven
   and is seated at the right hand
      of the Father.
He will come again in glory to judge
      the living and the dead
      and his kingdom will have no end.

I believe in the Holy Spirit, the Lord,
   the giver of life,
   who proceeds from the Father and the Son,
   who with the Father and the Son is
      adored and glorified,
   who has spoken through the prophets.
I believe in one, holy, catholic
   and apostolic Church.
I confess one Baptism for the
   forgiveness of sins
and I look forward to the resurrection of the
   dead and the life of the world to come.
Amen.

Praying with Mary

Jesus loved and honored his Mother. The Church has always loved and honored Mary. Mary trusted God completely. When asked to be the Mother of God's Son, she said: "May it be done to me according to your word" (Luke 1:38).

Memorare

Remember, most loving Virgin Mary,
never was it heard
that anyone who turned to you for help
was left unaided.
Inspired by this confidence,
though burdened by my sins,
I run to your protection
for you are my mother.
Mother of the Word of God,
do not despise my words of pleading
but be merciful and hear my prayer.
Amen.

Messengers of God

Aside from honoring Mary and the saints in prayer, we can also call on angels in prayer. Angels are creatures created by God as pure spirits. They do not have physical bodies. They serve God in his saving plan for us and constantly give him praise. Everyone has a guardian angel. We also recognize the Archangels Michael, Raphael, and Gabriel for their special roles as God's messengers in the Bible. We can ask the angels to help us in living as disciples of Jesus. Ask the angels to help you by praying the prayers below.

Angel of God

Angel of God,
my guardian dear,
to whom God's love
     commits me here,
ever this day be at my side,
to light and guard, to rule and guide.
Amen.

Prayer to Saint Michael the Archangel

Saint Michael the Archangel,
defend us in battle.
Be our defense against the wickedness
     and snares of the Devil.
May God rebuke him, we humbly pray, and
do thou,
O Prince of the heavenly hosts,
by the power of God,
thrust into hell Satan,
and all the evil spirits,
who prowl about the world
seeking the ruin of souls. Amen.

The Seven Themes of Catholic Social Teaching

Human dignity is the value and worth that come from being created in God's image and likeness. Jesus stood up for the human dignity of every person through his life and his teaching. Jesus' life and teaching are the foundation of Catholic social teaching. This teaching calls us to work for justice and peace as Jesus did. Discuss with your family ways in which you can work together for justice and peace.

1. **Life and Dignity of the Human Person** Human life is sacred because it is a gift from God. Because we are all God's children, we all share the same human dignity. As Christians we respect all people, even those we do not know.

2. **Call to Family, Community, and Participation** We are all social. We need to be with others to grow. The family is the basic community. In the family we grow and learn the values of our faith. As Christians we live those values in our family and community.

3. **Rights and Responsibilities of the Human Person** Every person has a fundamental right to life. This includes the things we need to have a decent life: faith and family, work and education, health care and housing. We also have a responsibility to others and to society. We work to make sure the rights of all people are being protected.

4. **Option for the Poor and Vulnerable** We have a special obligation to help those who are poor and in need. This includes those who cannot protect themselves because of their age or their health.

5. **Dignity of Work and the Rights of Workers** Our work is a sign of our participation in God's work. People have the right to decent work, just wages, safe working conditions, and to participate in decisions about work.

6. **Solidarity of the Human Family** Solidarity is a feeling of unity. It binds members of a group together. Each of us is a member of the one human family. The human family includes people of all racial and cultural backgrounds. We all suffer when one part of the human family suffers whether they live near or far away.

7. **Care for God's Creation** God created us to be stewards, or caretakers, of his creation. We must care for and respect the environment. We have to protect it for future generations. When we care for creation, we show respect for God the Creator.

Interfaith Dialogue

It seems just about every day we hear there is some tension or violence happening in our world among peoples of different faiths. Today more than ever, our communities are being pulled into emotional and sensitive dialogue, and it can be very difficult to find the right words for discussion or plan a path to healing. It should be as simple as mutual respect for each other's beliefs, but unfortunately, it is not. However, your family can look to our Church and the pope for answers. At the Second Vatican Council, the Catholic Church affirmed the Church's profound and abiding respect for other religions. The council stated that the Church "rejects nothing that is true and holy in these religions. She regards with sincere reverence those ways of conduct and of life, those precepts and teachings" (*Nostra Aetate*, 2).

New Commandment

"I give you a new commandment: love one another. As I have loved you . . . This is how all will know that you are my disciples, if you have love for one another."

John 13:34–35

Below are some important guidelines your family can remember when it comes to interfaith relationships and dialogues.

- The Church is a Christ-centered faith community.

- The Bible helps us think justly and morally about the world around us.

- Participation in the Church allows families to integrate faith into the culture of our lives.

- A commitment to Gospel values allows families to develop their faith formation and live fully as disciples of Christ.

Jesus gave us the New Commandment to help us follow the way he lived. It is especially applicable to interfaith dialogue. Read and talk about this commandment as a family. Let it guide all your interfaith relationships— at home, school, work, and in the community.

The Communion of Saints

One of the most comforting Catholic beliefs is our belief in the Communion of Saints. The Communion of Saints is the union of all baptized members of the Church on earth, in heaven, and in Purgatory. This belief is comforting because we remain united with our loved ones who have died and are all united with the saints in heaven, who intercede for us.

The Canonization Process

Have you or anyone in your family ever wondered how the Church decides who is named a saint? If someone who has died was known for living an especially holy life, or was martyred for his or her Catholic faith, the bishop of this person's diocese may begin the process to consider the person for sainthood. Here is a brief summary of this process.

- The first step is an investigation into the person's life. People who knew him or her are interviewed. The bishop collects information on what the person said, wrote, and did. The information is sent to the Vatican. When a person becomes a candidate for sainthood, he or she is known as "Servant of God."

- A group of cardinals at the Vatican, the Congregation for the Causes of Saints, studies the information about the candidate's life. They consider whether the person is a role model for living Catholic virtues. If so, the person can be declared "Venerable."

- The next step is declaring the candidate "Blessed." This is called "beatification." Beatification occurs if it can be shown that a miracle occurred in connection with the candidate or if the person died a martyr for the faith. An example of a miracle might be a sudden cure or healing, with no reasonable medical explanation, when someone prayed for the candidate's help. The Vatican carefully reviews the evidence on any miracles.

- If a second miracle can be credited to the candidate, he or she can be named "Saint," or canonized.

Litany of the Saints

Lord, have mercy.
Christ, have mercy.
Lord, have mercy.
Holy Mary, Mother of God,
    pray for us.
Saint Michael,
    pray for us.
Holy angels of God,
    pray for us.
Saint Peter and Saint Paul,
    pray for us.
Saint John,
    pray for us.
Saint Stephen,
    pray for us.
Saint Perpetua and Saint Felicity,
    pray for us.
Saint Prisca,
    pray for us.
Saint Gregory,
    pray for us.
Saint Augustine,
    pray for us.
Saint Basil,
    pray for us.
Saint Benedict,
    pray for us.
Saint Francis and Saint Dominic,
    pray for us.
Saint Catherine,
    pray for us.
Saint Teresa,
    pray for us.
All holy men and women,
    pray for us.
Lord, have mercy.
Christ, have mercy.
Lord, have mercy.

Glossary

Anointing of the Sick (page 90) the sacrament that gives God's grace and comfort to those who are sick

apostolic (page 54) a word describing how the Church is founded on the Apostles and passes down their teachings

Baptism (page 76) the sacrament in which we become members of the Church

Beatitudes (page 112) the teachings of Jesus that describe the way to live in God's happiness

bishop (page 96) ordained men who serve and lead the Church; bishops are successors of the Apostles

Blessed Trinity (page 30) God the Father, God the Son, and God the Holy Spirit are One God in Three Persons

catholic (page 54) universal; open to all people

common priesthood of the faithful (page 94) Christ's priestly mission, shared by all who are baptized

Communion of Saints (page 170) all of the baptized members of the Church, including baptized people living on earth and all who have died in God's love

compassion (page 113) the ability to understand and share in the feelings of another

Confirmation (page 80) the sacrament in which we are sealed with the Gift of the Holy Spirit

conscience (page 114) God's gift that helps us know right from wrong

covenant (page 20) an agreement between God and his people

deacon (page 96) ordained men who serve the Church by helping the bishop and priests

devotions (page 74) the many traditions, outside of the liturgy, that help us pray and show our love for God

Eucharist (page 81) the sacrament of Jesus' Body and Blood

glory (page 36) greatness or honor

Gospel (page 22) the Good News that we are saved by Jesus Christ, the Son of God

grace (page 137) our share in God's life and love

holy (pages 32, 54) growing in God's love and sharing it

Holy Orders (page 95) the sacrament in which baptized men are ordained to serve the Church as bishops, priests, and deacons

Incarnation (page 46) the mystery that the Son of God took on a human nature

justice (page 116) treating everyone fairly and with respect

Kingdom of God (page 181) the peace, love, and joy that Jesus brings us

liturgical year (page 72) the celebration throughout the year of the mysteries of Jesus' life and saving work

liturgy (page 62) the Church's participation in the saving work of Jesus Christ

Liturgy of the Hours (page 148) the official non-sacramental, communal prayer of the Church

Liturgy of the Word (page 71) the part of the Mass when we listen and respond to God's Word

Magisterium (page 124) the teaching office of the Church

Matrimony (page 97) the sacrament in which a baptized man and a baptized woman become husband and wife and promise to be faithful to each other for the rest of their lives; also called marriage

mortal sin (page 130) a very serious sin that breaks a person's relationship with God

natural law (page 108) God's wisdom, deep in our hearts, that guides us toward what is good

Oil of the Sick (page 90) holy oil that has been blessed by a bishop for use in Anointing of the Sick

one (page 54) a word that describes the Church as being the only Church that Jesus Christ founded

Original Sin (page 38) the first sin committed by Adam and Eve

Paschal Mystery (page 22) the Passion, Death, Resurrection, and Ascension of Jesus Christ

Penance and Reconciliation (page 86) the sacrament in which God is with us, forgiving our sins

petition (page 155) to ask for something

prayer (page 122) listening and talking to God

prayer of intercession (page 164) prayer asking for something on behalf of someone else

Precepts of the Church (page 124) laws to help us know our basic responsibilities as members of the Church

priests (page 96) ordained ministers who serve the Church by working with bishops to lead, teach, and celebrate the Eucharist and other sacraments

psalm (page 147) a prayer-song from the Bible that helps us to pray

Real Presence (page 82) the truth that the Risen Jesus—Body, Blood, soul, and divinity—is truly present in the Eucharist

Sacred Tradition (page 23) the ways the Church continues to pass on all that God revealed to us in Jesus Christ

sacramentals (page 66) blessings of people, actions, and religious objects that help us grow in faith and act on God's grace given in the sacraments

sacraments (page 64) special signs given to us by Jesus through which we receive God's grace

Sacraments at the Service of Communion (page 94) sacraments that strengthen people to serve God and the Church through the vocations of Matrimony or Holy Orders

Sacraments of Christian Initiation (page 78) the Sacraments of Baptism, Confirmation, and Eucharist, which make us part of the Church

sanctifying grace (page 139) the gift of God's life infused into our soul to heal us of sin and make us holy

sin (page 129) a thought, word, or action that is against God's law

Ten Commandments (page 120) God's laws that were given to Moses, to help people know how to love God and others

venial sin (page 130) a less serious sin that hurts a person's relationship with God

virtue (page 115) a good habit that helps us act according to God's love for us

worship (page 122) giving God thanks and praise

Q: What is the Gospel?

A: The Gospel is the Good News that we are saved by Jesus Christ, the Son of God. In the New Testament, the Gospels tell us about Jesus and his words and deeds. The Gospel writers are called the four Evangelists: Matthew, Mark, Luke, and John. *CCC, 73, 139, 561*

Q: What is Sacred Tradition?

A: Sacred Tradition is the Church's teaching of all that God revealed in Jesus Christ. Tradition includes creeds, or statements about what we believe. Along with Scripture, Tradition is inspired by the Holy Spirit. *CCC, 96, 97, 98*

Q: What is the Blessed Trinity?

A: The Blessed Trinity is God the Father, God the Son, and God the Holy Spirit as One God in Three Persons. The persons of the Blessed Trinity always existed and always will. The Blessed Trinity is a mystery at the heart of our faith. *CCC, 261, 267*

Q: What does it mean to be holy?

A: To be holy means to be growing in God's love and sharing it. When we are holy, we love God and are living in his love. The Holy Spirit helps us to grow in holiness. *CCC, 743, 747*

Q: What is glory?

A: Glory is God's goodness that is without end. All of creation takes part in God's glory. God wants us to share in this glory and live in his friendship. *CCC, 319, 353, 396*

Q: What is Original Sin?

A: Original Sin is the first sin committed by Adam and Eve. In the Bible, we learn that Original Sin is passed on to all people. Original Sin deprives us of the original holiness God intended for us. *CCC, 396, 416, 417, 418*

CCC = Catechism of the Catholic Church

Q: **Who is the Blessed Virgin?**

A: The Blessed Virgin is Mary, Jesus' mother. This title is given to her to honor her obedience and commitment to God's plan for her. It also teaches us that Mary did not have any other children. CCC, 509, 510

Q: **What is the Incarnation?**

A: The Incarnation is the mystery that the Son of God took on a human nature. CCC, 460, 479

Q: **What does the phrase one, holy, catholic, and apostolic mean?**

A: The phrase one, holy, catholic, and apostolic means that the Church is one because her source is one—the Blessed Trinity; it is holy because Christ is holy; it is universal, or open to all people; and its teachings are passed down to us from the Apostles. CCC, 865, 870

Q: **What are sacraments?**

A: Sacraments are special signs given to us by Jesus through which we receive God's grace. In each of the Seven Sacraments, we are granted a particular grace to make us holy. CCC, 1131

Q: **What is the liturgical year?**

A: The liturgical year is the Church's calendar that celebrates the events of Jesus' birth, life, Passion, Death, Resurrection, and Ascension throughout the year. CCC, 1095, 1168, 1171, 1194, 1349

Q: **What are the Sacraments of Christian Initiation?**

A: The Sacraments of Christian Initiation are the Sacraments of Baptism, Confirmation, and Eucharist that make us part of the Church. CCC, 1275

Q: **What is Baptism?**

A: This sacrament cleanses us of Original Sin and forgives any sins we have committed. We are welcomed into the Church and are called to be disciples. CCC, 1277, 1279, 1280

Q: **What is Confirmation?**

A: This sacrament strengthens our Baptism. We are sealed with the Gift of the Holy Spirit. *CCC, 1316, 1317, 1318*

Q: **What is Eucharist?**

A: In this sacrament, we receive Jesus' Body and Blood in Holy Communion. Receiving Holy Communion unites us more closely to Jesus and all the members of the Church. *CCC, 1407, 1409, 1413, 1414, 1416*

Q: **What is the Real Presence?**

A: The Real Presence is the truth that the Risen Jesus—Body, Blood, soul, and divinity—is truly present in the Eucharist. *CCC, 1416*

Q: **What is Penance and Reconciliation?**

A: Penance and Reconciliation is the Sacrament of Healing in which God is with us, forgiving our sins. We receive absolution, which means we are forgiven through the words and actions of the priest, in Jesus' name. *CCC, 1486, 1491*

Q: **What is Anointing of the Sick?**

A: Anointing of the Sick is the Sacrament of Healing that gives God's grace and comfort to those who are sick. In this sacrament, the priest prays on behalf of the whole Church, asking for God's help for the sick person. *CCC, 1527, 1531, 1532*

Q: **What is the common priesthood of the faithful?**

A: The common priesthood of the faithful means Christ's priestly mission, shared by all who are baptized. We share in Christ's mission of sacrifice and service to others. *CCC, 1591*

Q: **What is Holy Orders?**

A: Holy Orders is the sacrament in which baptized men are ordained to serve the Church as deacons, priests, and bishops. A bishop prays and lays hands on a man who is being ordained, just as the Apostles did. *CCC, 1593, 1597*

Q: **Who are bishops?**

A: Bishops are the successors of the Apostles who lead the Church. They usually lead and care for large communities called dioceses. *CCC, 1594, 1595, 1596*

Q: Who are priests?

A: Priests are ordained ministers who serve the Church by working with bishops to lead, teach, and celebrate the Eucharist and other sacraments. *CCC, 1565–1568*

Q: Who are deacons?

A: Deacons are men who have received the Sacrament of Holy Orders to serve the Church by helping the bishop and priests. *CCC, 1569, 1570, 1571*

Q: What is Matrimony?

A: Matrimony is the sacrament in which a baptized man and a baptized woman become husband and wife and promise to be faithful to each other for the rest of their lives. Matrimony is also called marriage. *CCC, 1658, 1660, 1661*

Q: What is natural law?

A: Natural law is God's wisdom, deep in our hearts, that guides us toward what is good. When we live by following God's natural law, we are doing what God wants for us. *CCC, 1978, 1979*

Q: What are the Beatitudes?

A: The Beatitudes are the teachings of Jesus that describe the way to live in God's happiness. *CCC, 1715, 1726*

Q: What is conscience?

A: Conscience is a gift from God that helps us know right from wrong. We form our conscience through practice and study of the faith. *CCC, 1799*

Q: What is a virtue?

A: A virtue is a good habit that helps us act according to God's love for us. The more good that we do, the easier it is for us to live in God's love and happiness. *CCC, 1840*

Q: What is justice?

A: Justice means treating everyone fairly and with respect. *CCC, 1926, 1943*

Q: What are the Ten Commandments?

A: The Ten Commandments are God's laws that were given to Moses, to help people know how to love God and others. *CCC, 1980, 1983*

Q: What are prayer and worship?

A: Prayer is listening and talking to God with our minds and hearts. When we pray, we can grow closer to God. Worship is giving God thanks and praise. We adore God and thank him for his many gifts. *CCC, 2135*

Q: What is the Magisterium?

A: The Magisterium is the teaching office of the Church. It is how the Church teaches and guides us in the truth. *CCC, 2051*

Q: What are the Precepts of the Church?

A: The Precepts of the Church are laws given to us to help us know our basic responsibilities as members of the Church. *CCC, 2047, 2048*

Q: What is sin?

A: Sin is a thought, word, or action that is against God's law. When we sin, we harm our relationship with God and with one another. We also hurt ourselves. *CCC, 1872*

Q: What is mortal sin?

A: Mortal sin is a very serious sin that breaks a person's relationship with God. *CCC, 1854–1861*

Q: What is venial sin?

A: Venial sin is a less serious sin that hurts a person's relationship with God. *CCC, 1874, 1875*

Q: What is grace?

A: Grace is our share in God's life and love. It strengthens us to live as Jesus' disciples. *CCC, 2027*

Q: What is sanctifying grace?

A: Sanctifying grace is the gift of God's life infused into our soul to heal us of sin and make us holy. *CCC, 2020*

Q: **What is prayer?**

A: Prayer is listening and talking to God. We can pray at any time and in any place. We can pray aloud or in silence. We can pray by ourselves or with others. The celebration of the Mass is the Church's greatest prayer. *CCC, 2590*

Q: **What is the Communion of Saints?**

A: The Communion of Saints is all of the baptized members of the Church, including baptized people living on earth and all who have died in God's love. *CCC, 960, 1053, 1054*

Q: **What is the season of Advent?**

A: Advent is a season of hope. God promised to send his Son to save us. Jesus came to show us the Father's love. In Advent, we wait in joyful hope to celebrate the birth of Jesus. *CCC, 524*

Q: **What does Jesus give to us by his birth on Christmas?**

A: The birth of Jesus on Christmas is a sign of hope. We have hope because Jesus came to save us. The Church celebrates Jesus as a sign of hope at Christmas and all year long. *CCC, 525, 529*

Q: **What does the season of Lent remind us of?**

A: Lent reminds us that Jesus gave his life for us on the Cross. He did this out of love for all people. *CCC, 540*

Q: **What do we remember during the Triduum?**

A: During the Triduum, we recall Jesus' suffering and Death and celebrate his Resurrection. *CCC, 1168*

Q: **What do we celebrate at Easter?**

A: Easter is a celebration of Jesus' Resurrection, but it is also a season to remember God's gift of the Church. The Church proclaims the Good News so that all people can come to know the Risen Christ. *CCC, 640, 1076*

Index

A

Absolution, 87

Adam, 38

Advent, 72, 165, 193–198

Alberto Hurtado (Saint), 167

Alphonsus Liguori (Saint), 125

Altar Diagram, 244–245

Angels, 44, 52, 62, 81, 156, 171, 172, 201, 203, 220

Anne-Marie Javouhey (Blessed), 109

Anne Mary Taigi (Blessed), 133

Anointing of the Sick, 56, 65, 85, 86, 90

Apostles, 23, 24, 51, 52, 54, 55–56, 95–96, 136, 140, 157, 163, 219

Apostles' Creed, 37, 51, 238

Apostolic, 54–55

Augustine (Saint), 41

B

Baptism, 52, 65, 66, 78–79, 94, 107, 140, 213
   Church membership through, 52, 78–79, 94, 107
   Sacrament of, 65, 66
   sanctifying grace through, 140
   Triduum, 213

Beatitudes, 112, 120

Benedict (Saint), 141

Benedict XVI (Pope), 177

Bible. *See also* Scripture
   as God's Word, 21–22, 27
   knowing God from, 19

Bishop of Rome (Pope), 56, 96

Bishops, 55–56, 95–96

Blessed
   Anne-Marie Javouhey, 109
   Anne Mary Taigi, 133
   Pier Giorgio Frassati, 117
   Stanley Rother, 99

Blessed Trinity, 30–32, 154

Blessed Virgin, 45

Body and Blood of Christ, 53, 63, 77, 146, 158

C

Catholic, 54, 73

Catholic social teaching, 116

Charity, 115

Chrism, 94

Christian Initiation, Sacraments of, 77, 78

Christmas, 72, 199–204

Church
   Advent, 193–198
   as Body of Christ, 24
   calendar of, 69, 70, 72
   Christmas, 199–204
   communion of holy, faithful people, 170
   definition of, 51–57
   helps us live in God's friendship, 39
   of the home, 98
   knowing God through, 19, 29
   liturgy of, 165, 171
   members of, 77, 89
   one, holy, catholic, apostolic, 54
   prayers of, 146, 150, 158, 162–165
   Precepts of, 124
   sacraments of, 104
   works for justice and peace, 116

Church year, 187–192
   Prayer Ritual, 190–191

Common priesthood of the faithful, 94

Communion of Saints, 170

Compassion, 113

Confession, 87, 132

Confirmation, 65, 78, 80, 94

Conscience, 114

Contrition, 87

Covenant, 20

Creation, 28, 36

Creeds, 37, 51, 238, 252

Cross, 207

Crucifixes, 66

D

David (King), 147

Deacons, 56, 95–96

Devotions, 74

Dioceses, 56, 96

The Disciples Spread the Good News of Jesus, 226–227

Dominic Savio (Saint), 67

E

Easter, 217–222

Edith Stein (Saint), 159

Elijah, 136

Eternal, 39

Eucharist, 81–82
    celebration of, 47, 71
    Christian Initiation, 78
    Communion of Saints, 170
    drawing people closer to God, 149
    importance of, 156
    Liturgy of, 63, 189
    prayer in, 146, 158, 171
    Sacrament, 65, 77, 78
    Eve, 38

F

Faith, 35
    as gift from God, 37
    supporting prayer, 174
    virtue of, 115

Families, first school of prayer, 173

Forgiveness, 40, 81, 85–92, 101, 129

Freedom, 107

Free will, 107, 128

G

Gathering Prayer, 188, 194, 200, 206, 212, 218, 224, 230

Genuflecting, 66

Gertrude the Great (Saint), 151

Glory, 36

God
    as Blessed Trinity, 30–32
    as Creator, 19–20, 35–41
    as Father, Son, and Holy Spirit, 27
    glory of, 36
    grace of, 104, 112, 135, 136–138
    honoring him, 121
    Kingdom of, 181, 231
    knowing him, 27–34
    Lord's Prayer unites people with, 179
    love of, 22, 29, 30, 32, 38–40, 47, 62, 64, 70, 85, 88, 89, 103–110, 111–118, 128
    mercy of, 139
    prayer brings us closer to, 149
    relationship with through prayer, 146–150
    sin damaging relationship with, 129–130
    virtues from, 115

God's Word, 114

Good News, 22

Gospels, 22, 71. *See also* John (Gospel); Luke (Gospel); Mark (Gospel); Matthew (Gospel); Scripture

Grace, 137
    bringing healing and holiness, 138
    free gift of God, 137
    the power of, 254
    sanctifying, 139–140

Gregorian chant, 75

Gregory the Great (Saint), 75

H

Healing
    Sacraments of, 85
    through grace, 138

Hogar de Cristo, 167

Holiness, 138

Holy, 32, 54

Holy candles, 66

Holy Communion, 53, 78, 82, 250

Holy Days of Obligation, 124

Holy Family, 45

Holy oil, 94

Holy Orders, 65, 94, 95–96

Holy Spirit
    as Advocate, 32
    grace from, 107
    as guide, 21, 53, 63, 112, 219
    guiding prayer, 149, 154, 158, 171

inspiring traditions, 24

leading us to grace, 137

as Third Person of the Blessed Trinity, 27, 30–32

at Pentecost, 23, 72, 223–228

prepared Mary, 44–45

sanctifying grace from, 139

Holy water, 66

Homily, 71, 77

Hope, 115

I

Incarnation, 46

Intercession, 51–57, 93–99, 161–168

Intercession, prayer of, 164

J

James (Saint), 136

Jesus Appears to Mary Magdalene, 220–221

Jesus Christ

Advent, 193–198

Ascension of, 72, 138

baptism of, 27

Beatitudes from, 112, 120

Birth of, 46, 72, 199–204

Bread of Life, 53

Death of, 47, 138, 207, 213

as Head of the Church, 52–53

healing and forgiveness from, 85–91

hope from, 201

Incarnation of, 46

knowing God through, 19

Lord's Prayer unites people with, 179

modeling God's love, 46

as model of holiness, 231

as Second Person of the Blessed Trinity, 30–32

prayer and, 62, 148, 150

Resurrection of, 48, 72, 138, 217–222

return of, 48

sacraments from, 64

sanctifying grace through, 135

as Savior, 22, 43

sharing love, 63

Transfiguration of, 136–137, 139

John (Gospel), 22

John (Saint), 136

John the Baptist, 196–197

John the Baptist (Saint), 31, 33, 72, 196–197

John Bosco (Saint), 67, 183

Joseph (Saint), 49

Julian of Norwich, 175

Justice, 116

K

Katharine Drexel (Saint), 83

Kingdom of God, 181, 231

L

Last Supper, 81–82, 105, 157

Lectio and *Visio Divina*, 27–34, 85–91, 135–142, 169–176

Lent, 165, 205–210

Prayer Ritual, 208–209

Litany, 43–49

Liturgical year, 69, 70, 72, 187–234

Liturgy, 62–63, 65, 69, 153–154

Liturgy of the Eucharist, 63, 65, 71, 77, 78

Liturgy of the Hours, 165

Liturgy of the Word, 71, 72

Lord's Day, 70–71, 122

Lord's Prayer, 177–184

Love

acts of, 83

for God, 28, 74, 111–118, 122, 124

God's, 20–21, 22, 29, 30, 32, 38–40, 47, 62, 64, 70, 85, 87, 88, 89, 103–110, 128

at home, 98

Jesus Christ's, 46, 63, 77, 93

in matrimony, 97

turning away from, 127–132

Luke (Gospel), 22

M

Magi, 201, 202–203

Magisterium, 121, 124

Mark (Gospel), 22

Mary

as disciple, 45

Holy Spirit prepared, 44–45

honoring, 74

Mother of God, 44–45

Mother of Jesus, 31, 43, 62
  Praying with, 257
Mass
  to celebrate Lord's Day, 70–71, 122
  celebration of, 40, 56, 62
  Communion of Saints, 170
  Eucharist as, 82
  Penitential Act, 156
  prayer in, 146, 162, 172
  on Sunday, 122
Matrimony, 65, 94, 97
Matthew (Gospel), 22, 25
Medals, 66
Meditation, 61–67, 119–126
Messengers of God, 253
Missionary discipleship, 18, 60, 102, 144, 186
Monica (Saint), 41
Mortal sin, 130–131
Moses, 136

N

Natural law, 108
New Testament, 63, 71
Nicene Creed, 252
Nicholas (Saint), 57

O

Oil of the Sick, 90
Old Testament, 63, 71
One Church community, 54
Order of Confirmation, 80
Ordinary Time, 72, 229–234
  Prayer Ritual, 232–233
Original Sin, 38, 78, 79, 127, 128

P

Padre Pio (Saint), 91
Partners in Faith
  Alberto Hurtado, 167
  Alphonsus Liguori (Saint), 125
  Anne-Marie Javouhey, 109
  Anne Mary Taigi, 133
  Augustine (Saint), 41
  Benedict (Saint), 141
  Dominic Savio (Saint), 67

  Edith Stein (Saint), 159
  Gertrude the Great (Saint), 151
  Gregory the Great, (Saint) 75
  John Bosco (Saint), 183
  John the Baptist (Saint), 33
  Joseph (Saint), 49
  Julian of Norwich, 175
  Katharine Drexel (Saint), 83
  Nicholas (Saint), 57
  Padre Pio (Saint), 91
  Pier Giorgio Frassati, 117
  Pierre Toussaint, 18, 25, 60, 102, 144, 186
  Stanley Rother, 99
Passover meal, 81
Paul (Saint), 51, 52, 163
Peace, 116
Penance, 87
Penance and Reconciliation, 40, 56, 65, 85, 86–89,
  128, 129, 165, 252
Penitential Act, 156
Pentecost, 23, 55, 72, 223–228
People
  caring for each other, 105–106
  conscience of, 114
  created in God's image, 103–110
  free will, 107, 128
  glorify God with Lord's Prayer, 180
  God's gifts to, 104
  in God's image, 116, 128
  love one another, 116, 119
  putting God first, 113
  respect, 106
  responding to God's love, 111–118
Perseverance, 163
Peter (Saint), 51, 52, 55, 96, 136
Petition, 127–134, 153–160
Pier Giorgio Frassati (Blessed), 117
Pierre Toussaint (Venerable), 18, 25, 60,
  102, 144, 186
Pilgrimage, 74
Pope, 55–56, 96
Pope Benedict XVI, 177
Praise, 35–41, 145–152
Prayer, 145–152
  Act of Contrition, 237

Apostles' Creed, 37, 51, 238
of blessing, 162
building trust in God through, 155–156
of the Church, 147, 162–165, 171–172
Church Year Prayer Ritual, 190–191
Confiteor, 156
different ways to, 161
Evening Prayer, 237
of the Faithful, 164
Gathering, 188, 194, 200, 206, 212, 218, 224, 230
gift from God, 114
Glory Be to the Father, 236
Grace After Meals, 238
Grace Before Meals, 173, 238
Hail, Holy Queen, 238
of intercession, 164
Lent Prayer Ritual, 208–209
liturgy as, 62
Lord's Prayer, 177–184
Ordinary Time Prayer Ritual, 232–233
Our Father, 236
as part of Sacred tradition, 153–154
of praise, 162
Rosary, 74, 239
of Saint Benedict, 237
Sign of the Cross, 63, 236
supporting faith, 174
talking to God, 122
Triduum Prayer Ritual, 214–215
Precepts of the Church, 124
Priests, 56, 95–96
Processions, 74
Prophets, 94, 172
Psalm, 147–148

R

Rainbow, 20
Readers Theater
The Disciples Spread the Good News of Jesus, 226–227
Jesus Appears to Mary Magdalene, 220–221
John the Baptist, 196–197
A Visit from the Magi, 202–203
Real Presence, 82
Reasoning, 114
Reconciliation. *See* Penance and Reconciliation

Repentance, 87
Resurrection, 48, 72, 138, 217–222
Revelations of Divine Love, 175
Risen Christ, 219
Rite of Penance, 89
Roman Missal
Confiteor, 156
Eucharistic Prayer 2, 169
Mystery of Faith, 43
Penitential Act, 127
Prayer asking God's help, 162
Prayers of blessing, 162
Prayers of praise, 162
Sanctus, 171–172
Rosary, 66, 74, 239

S

Sabbath, 121, 122
Sacramentals, 66, 207, 250
Sacraments, 64–65. *See also* Anointing of the Sick;
    Baptism; Confirmation; Eucharist; Holy
    Orders; Matrimony; Penance and
    Reconciliation
Body and Blood of Christ, 146
of Christian Initiation, 77, 78
of Healing, 85–91
Holy Communion, 53
at the Service of Communion, 93, 94
as signs given by Jesus, 61, 64
Sacred Scripture, 21–22, 63
Sacred Tradition, 23–24, 153–154
Saints. *See also* Partners in Faith
    Alberto Hurtado, 167
    Alphonsus Liguori, 125
    Augustine, 41
    Benedict, 141
    celebration of, 74
    Dominic Savio, 67
    Edith Stein, 159
    Gertrude the Great, 151
    Gregory the Great, 75
    James, 136
    John, 136
    John the Baptist, 31, 33, 72, 196–197
    John Bosco, 67, 183
    Joseph, 49
    Katharine Drexel, 83

Monica, 41

Nicholas, 57

Padre Pio, 91

Paul, 51, 52, 163

Peter, 51, 52, 55, 96, 136

Sanctifying grace, 135, 139–140

Scripture. *See also* Bible

   1 Corinthians, 89

   1 John, 132

   1 Peter, 211

   Acts of the Apostles, 23, 48, 135, 157, 217, 219, 223, 226–227

   Colossians, 163

   Exodus, 120

   Genesis, 19, 69, 97, 121

   James, 103, 153

   John, 31, 35, 39, 47, 51, 53, 97, 105, 111, 157, 220–221

   Luke, 44, 46, 81, 86, 88, 93, 178, 199

   Mark, 155, 196–197

   Matthew, 25, 32, 55, 61, 64, 70, 81, 112, 113, 136, 172, 187, 202–203

   Philippians, 161, 229

   Psalm, 147, 148, 149, 205

   Revelations, 193

   Romans, 119

Service, 105–106

Service of Communion, Sacraments at the, 93, 94

   Holy Orders, 65, 93, 94, 95–96

   Matrimony, 65, 93, 94, 97

Seven themes of Catholic social teaching, 258

Shepherds, 201

Sign of the Cross, 63, 66, 150, 190, 206, 208, 233

Silent prayers, 166

Sin, 129

   confessing, 132

   mortal, 130–131

   Original, 38, 127, 128

   venial, 130

Souls, 39

Stanley Rother (Blessed), 99

Stations of the Cross, 74, 207, 247

Statues, 66

Stigmata, 91

Sunday, 70–71, 122

Sunday Mass, 122, 165

T

Ten Commandments, 119, 120, 122–123, 242, 249

Thanksgiving, 69–75, 77–83, 103–110

Traditional, prayer, 19–26, 177–184

Transfiguration, 136–137, 139

Triduum, 211–216

   Prayer Ritual, 214–215

U

Unit Prayer, 18, 60, 102, 144, 186

V

Venial sin, 130

Virtues, 115, 131

A Visit from the Magi, 202–203

W

Witnesses, 80

Word of God, 154

Worship, 122